Be Blessed

You say; "I'm not able."

God says: "I am able."

May God's Holy Spirit lead and guide you!!

May Jesus' Holy Light light up your world!!

Lottie Gillmore

Supernatural Flying Monkeys and Dancing Chickens

LOTTIE GILLMORE

authorHOUSE®

AuthorHouse™
1663 Liberty Drive
Bloomington, IN 47403
www.authorhouse.com
Phone: 1-800-839-8640

© 2009 Lottie Gillmore. All rights reserved.

No part of this book may be reproduced, stored in a retrieval system, or transmitted by any means without the written permission of the author.

First published by AuthorHouse   5/26/2009

ISBN: 978-1-4389-6836-0 (sc)

Printed in the United States of America
Bloomington, Indiana

This book is printed on acid-free paper.

Prelude

Supernatural

"Flying Monkeys and Dancing Chickens"

Welcome to my sincere, personal, life testimony and journey, as I, Elizabeth Storres, unveil extreme tragedy in the form of emotional and physical abuse from an alcoholic father and a life, starting at six years old, of the silent thief, Multiple Sclerosis, that tried to steel my healthy mother from me and my brother, Jonathan.

As a little child, I never knew anything else except extreme poverty, drunkenness and physical helplessness, for my mother, my brother, even my dad and last but not least, me, Elizabeth. The tragedies that loomed over us were like that of sticky, black tar fog, which I now call "Flying Monkeys".

As our daily toxic "Flying Monkeys" seemed to try to wipe our family off the face of the earth, years later still deeply scarred wounds of these memories, bring forth in me, tears of great pain.

After, somehow, reaching sweet seventeen, I made a decision, that actually could have in the years to come, suck me out of this world and into the very pits of Hell. That decision was to marry a man named Murrey, in high hopes, of shedding the ongoing ugliness, of my then present, young life. I was actually making a flying leap from a very scolding frying pan to the unquenchable fire of his Hell, trying desperately to escape my families' poverty and sickness.

Being married for eleven years, I lived with little or no love until God the Father gave to me a beautiful gift, that being Jesus Christ, who actually Saved me, supernaturally, from physical death.

As the Grace and Love of God, that the Father is, my life's sour situation made a 180 degree turnabout the moment I asked "Jesus Christ" into my heart and life!

Remember, we all "do" have a choice to make; that choice being "life or death?" Twenty four years ago, I chose "life" and now I believe I am called to tell my true amazing story. At times it is quite disturbing and at other times it is nothing short of "miraculous!"

As you search these revealing pages, may God the Father, supernaturally lead, guide and bless you abundantly!

From the Bottom of My Heart,
Elizabeth Storres

This Book is Dedicated
To
My Dear, Loving, Best Friend
Husband
Corneileous Jackobus
Who Shares My Heart's Dreams

And to
My Match Making, Life-long Friend

Gail Barbara
Who Introduced My Husband and Me Together

Love You Both

Supernatural

Flying Monkeys and Dancing Chickens

The world keeps turning, people die and babies are born. Many people, around the world, consider the birth of a child a true miracle. Only God knows for sure how a tiny seed can produce something so alive and complex. When one is born the end of the journey is surely dying. As many people can testify, sometimes we are given a second chance at life and living. Daily as we journey there are things that are not so great and at times things that are wonderful. Now the "not so good" things could be called "flying monkeys" and the very good things could be called "dancing chickens. I've had my share of both, as has everyone, around the globe.

Looking into a person's heart and mind you will find a multitude of pages, many chapters and finally a unique book that will amaze you.

As a "born again" believer, I, Elizabeth, would like to take you on a journey that will give you some insight as to whether or not you believe in "Flying Monkey's and Dancing Chicken's". You be the judge.

First I would like to inject that in no way, shape or form is this book meant to disrespect or dishonor any person mentioned. I believe people are put in our lives for a reason, season or perhaps just a fleeting moment.

This story is meant to be my testimony of God's miracles or "dancing chickens" that through constant prayer, faith and trusting, God, overcome life's numerous treacherous negative hurdles, "Flying Monkey's". With Jesus in our hearts, minds and souls, we as believers can and do overcome obstacles and are many times rescued, sometimes even from deaths door, therefore "Saved". We all have an eternity to someday fulfill and from what my journey through life has taught me, I choose to fulfill my eternity in the City of Heaven.

Chapter 1

March 1957

As you can see, I was born quite a long time ago, into a family of German decent. I arrived in the "old" hospital in this small southern Alberta city. My parents, Gertie and Lenard, farmed just out of a small community some thirty miles away. The fact that my mother has conceived a child at-all was perhaps my first "dancing chicken", as my parent's had been married a full eight year's before my precious birth took place.

My mother, at the age of fourteen, had been hospitalized with a ruptured appendix. She almost died from the poison in her body and after a six month hospital stay in the hospital her young body slowly regained a measure of health. The doctor informed her parents that she may never be able to conceive a child. Little did the doctor know that "Jesus" was in the mother and father of that young fourteen year old and "Miracle's" do "happen".

My Mom and Dad were raised in the same farming

community and met at a country dance. Following a short courtship they were married. Having come from a God loving home it was hard to reconcile why my Dad began to smoke and drink. Although Gertie was very hurt by her husband's drunken spree's, she remained extremely calm and quiet, always considerate, she just kept on doing her best to cope with the drinking and the poverty, then, and for many years to come.

Chapter 2

Our little family lived on the farm for the first month of my life, but then came a big decision to move the "city", for then the Storres family moved to a basement suite in the city. My parents must have thought life would be better and easier for all of us in a larger community. Life went on and life was mostly good. My dad drove big truck's, my mom cleaned a motel, while, I just grew, played and one great day learned to tie my own shoelaces.

Sometimes on hot summer days, two of my aunts would walk to our house bringing with them ice cream to share and enjoy. That was so much fun and a rare treat. Our house was on the crest of a very large hill and on those hot summer days my swimming hole was a big round, metal bucket in the front yard. In my three year-old innocence, there was many a day I would role down that hill giggling all the while, only to drop, about two feet, onto the sidewalk below.

Amazingly, there were no cracked or broken bones in this crazy event. I was also very proud to be able to put one leg, at a time, behind my neck. Ouch! I guess you could say I was somewhat bendable.

At three year's old, my dad would play a little game with me. Mom in her chair and dad in his, both in the small living room, would get quite entertained, as my dad would ask me to go back behind his chair into a dark kitchen, to retrieve his cigarettes. As I was inside the very dark, windowless kitchen, my dad would then proceed to exclaim, strongly and loudly, that the "boogie-man" was going to get me! With extreme fear and anxiety, I would turn around and as fast as my little legs would take me, flee back into the light and the safety of my parent's presence! This sometimes went on for what seemed a very long time. Even at three years old, I wanted to be a "pleaser" and "helpful". Not once did my dad or mom ever think that this "little game" would be a source of fear, for me, for the rest of my life.

Through the years, my dad just kept on drinking, it didn't get better and it didn't get worse. It was just always there. Of course at three, I was clueless about such things.

For my fourth birthday, mom and I shared a beautifully decorated cake. My mom's birthday was the day after mine and for many years to come we celebrated together. At the age of four, we got our first black and white TV set. Wow! We enjoyed it so much together in that little basement suite, where we stayed until I was five.

Chapter 3

1961 – Mom, dad and I were on the move again, this time to another basement suite, but on the S.W. Hill, closer to the schools. Little did this small family know of the new and quite tragic, events that were about to unfold.

In 1963 I started school, made new friend's on the block and learned to ride a two-wheeler, banana seat, streamer's and all. However, two of the biggest event's while being six year's old was the wonderful event of a little baby brother, Jonathan and the terrifying news of a horrible disease, coming into our home, via my soft spoken mother, called Multiple Sclerosis. My dear soft spoken mom, at thirty-four years young, was about to undergo some drastic changes in her life. Her life and that of each family member would never be the same.

Day after day, month after month, life went on, I'd be playing dress up and make- believe while the core of our family life was teetering on a very fragile axis. Our home life stricken with alcohol abuse, emotional and physical sickness, but this little girl thankfully never once recognized their aching poverty. It was just the way life happened.

My physically ill mother quit her cleaning position at the motel as she was unable to cope with the day to day physical demands of the job. My emotionally ill father just kept on drinking, weekends.

The bright spot was that little Jonathan was a sweet, healthy, adorable baby brother, who also was considered a precious miracle by many family members. Now there were two offspring, where none had been expected. It seemed that with all the "flying monkey's" in this household, there were also a few badly needed "dancing chicken's" in the middle of everything.

Chapter 4

With dad imbibing alcohol every weekend, we saw him falling down the stairs, a hurtful experience, but my father successfully lived through each incident with seemingly, no ill effect to his person. Not only was there "flying monkey's", mom and the kid's, saw the man of the house trying to "fly" as well. Wonder upon wonders, he didn't break his neck or anything else, for that matter. I didn't realize at that tender age that my father, was a very sick man. It seemed like he could not accept or cope with what life had in store for him, which made it hard to keep promises to his little girl. The same man that was so out of control on weekends was during the week, the funniest, kindest, most caring and loving social man, you could ever ask to meet.

At six year's old, this little Elizabeth didn't know anything about emotional sickness and what it can do to a person or the family. I only knew the pain in my heart was beginning to become too big a burden for one so small.

The emotional pain was enormous for my mother as

well, while dealing with alcohol abuse, poverty, and now a life-long sentence of MS she was beaten down by life's circumstances. In all those years my stubborn mother took no drugs, no vitamins nor any kind of supplements. She quietly and courageously took the best possible care of her family but was never able to say those words my childish heart longed to hear, "I love you, Elizabeth". Her own emotional plate was overflowing but she never voiced it. With steady, constant actions this "silent hero" soldiered on year after year without a complaint.

Chapter 5

Although I was only six, something quite incredible happened to me that I sure wasn't expecting. While sound asleep one summer night, I believe I was given a glimpse into what felt and seemed incredibly real. In the dream, it seemed God allowed me to peek, up and into a room, something like a class- room, with many rows of empty desk's. There I saw one lonely, white figure in the room and I had the sense that it was me, waiting to be born. When I awoke, I felt strongly like I had just been shown from where I had come from, before birth. Then as a young child and now as a grandmother, the experience was incredibly real.

Looking back over a life full of "flying monkey's" I believe God knew I would need His assurance, at that very young and tender hearted age. Through many life trials, I now know His promise, that "He will never leave us or forsake us", Hebrews 13:5, is very true.

After having this eye opening encounter with Heaven, I retained the belief throughout my life, that no matter what tragedies or "flying monkey's" that plague my pathway, the God of the universe, has His Great and Mighty Hand on the whole course of action.

Chapter 6

We know children seem to go through a period of time when, very early in life, a youngster will yell at a parent or stick out their tongue in defiance. In 1963, children were still to be seen and not heard. There was much less rudeness by adults and certainly children were risking a thrashing if they got out of line.

However, as my days were torn by broken promises, alcohol abuse and undeniable family physical sickness blended with poverty, I felt my father was one day Jeckle and the next day Hyde. I loved him so much when he was sober and bitterly hated him when he was drunk. I never knew for sure whose knee I was about to sit on, was it my dads knee or that of the drunk. One night, before bedtime I blurted out in painful tears, to my drunken dad, that I hated him and hoped he would die. Actually, it was only the "drunken" dad that I hated. Thus started year's of conscience anxiety, possibly for my father, but definitely for me.

As my mother coped with her threatening disease and a

busy, bouncing baby boy, she also was tempted to leave behind, at least, some of the misery in her life, that being her husband. At that time in her life the cards were stacked very high "against" her indeed. If she decided to stay, she would have to "shut up and put up" with any and all of her husband's behavior, sane, insane, drunk or sober. If she left, how would she be able to take care of two young children? Mother had two sisters that would have helped her, but the enormity of caring for her children and the possibility of greater illness loomed on the horizon, persuaded her to remain. Dad won out and our family stayed together. God knew what this young family was heading for and by the Grace of God, we didn't.

Chapter 7

Thank goodness for school, grade one, teachers and yes, a friend, Nancy. Grade one was blessed with a caring, loving home room teacher. Mrs. Romfo was gentle, calm, pretty and showed great kindness with every word she spoke to me and others. Nancy, a girl from down the street, became my best friend and we were soon inseparable. We played and played. We walked to school together, as I would call on her every morning on our daily trek.

Just before Christmas, Nancy asked me over to her house for a sleep over. I was so excited but also somewhat anxious. The next morning I was totally horrified when my dear friend, quietly and tenderly told me that I smelled… bad. Kids are noted for being honest but never before did anyone tell me or even suggest, to me, that I was dirty. Even at that young age, I was so humiliated that I wished I could crawl under the nearest rock.

Actually, when I was growing up, a bath was not a regular occurrence for me and at many times, throughout childhood, I had dirty feet and ankles. With such poverty, sickness and emotional turmoil looming thickly over our family, I am sure, God saw the shameful, heart-rendering circumstances and has, with His love, forgiven my two hurting, broken parent's.

Walking threw strife and heartache, for much of my life, my heart holds only understanding, love and forgiveness for my two, very down to earth, parents. They did the best they could by the only means they had.

As a stay at home mom, my mother was also seeing doctors regularly, at least for awhile, while Jonathan was growing. Jonathan was getting bigger and heavier and harder for mom to handle. With Jonathan six year's younger than me, we actually never really "played", but in year's to come we became very close and dear to each other

Chapter 8

In 1965, our growing family made our last residence move before I left home. We moved into an 800 sq. foot house when I was eight and Jonathan was two. Just about that time my dad, Lenard got a new position with a local retailer in town, driving their delivery truck. Gertie, my mother, became more and more afflicted with her medical "flying monkey" MS.

One summer afternoon, at ten years old, I was sitting on the back steps with one of my friends discussing my mother's health condition. We didn't have a lot of knowledge but as we talked about my mom's MS progression, I naturally thought she would be in a wheelchair in the next few years. She was still walking but with great unbalance and effort, holding onto walls, fences, etc. as she went. She had been diagnosed two years earlier but as "dancing chickens" would have it and with mother's grit, it would be twenty years before she was wheelchair bound.

Even though this family was so dysfunctional we still tried to live as normal as normal a life as possible. I don't know how but my father was able to buy a small tent-trailer, which frankly, was a source of sanity for each family member. Mom, dad, Jonathan, Sparky, the family dog, and I, would on summer weekends, pile in the car and head for a lake nearby. It certainly was a huge relief from regular drunken bouts that caused such stress and pressure. I have looked back many times, over the years, in awe and thanked God with great appreciation, for this blessing and that little "dancing chicken" tent-trailer for me and our family to enjoy. Truly the long arm of God was helping us through the difficult times. Hard as it was at times, I held strongly, an undeniable place in my heart for my savior, Jesus, as He was undeniably in my heart. On a couple of occasions, while camping, there came about incidents that were considered near-misses, but by the Grace of God, no one was hurt. Again camping out at Rattlesnake Dam, our family set up camp with our tiny, two bed, tent-trailer. With night time approaching, hurricane-like winds starting to howl, our miniature house was almost flung head first into the vast body of water. With the wind picking it up and turning it over like a top, it landed yards away like that of a kite just crashing to the ground.

Dad chased it frantically, as it lifted and started to half skim, half fly uncontrollably towards the body of water. Out of breath from fighting the wind and running wildly, dad grabbed it and drug the sorry thing back to the car. Again, we witnessed another "dancing chicken". We were scared but very, very happy!

By God's mercy, our family had not yet settled down for the night inside it and all were unharmed. Soon the unit was re-hooked onto the back of the car: mom, dad, dog and kids, were packed into the vehicle: and as late as it was, summer storm and all: away we inched back to safer territory.

On another camping excursion in the middle of the BC Mountains, another scary event, yet happy outcome, unfolded. This time our family had the uneasy fear of being mauled or eaten by a mountain bear during the late hours of the night.

Dark had draped the air and all were ready for bed. Earlier on the trip, mom and dad had warned us kids to properly use a garbage bag for any unused food scraps or wrappers we had. As Jonathan was tucked in with dad and I was cozy in bed with mom we retired for the night telling stories of "real live" bears. Barely had we closed our tired eyes when our ears took over. Bang, crash, bang, rustle and bang again. Jonathan and I certainly didn't need any more bear stories as one was unfolding right outside our tent-trailer, as we lay paralyzed with fear.

Sparky, almost had a fit barking and whining. As mom, had difficulty walking, let alone running for safety, we stayed put, listening in fear to all the noise. As always, dad had a load of beer in his belly. Again, Please God, No! Once again, our lives were teetering on the brink of disaster!

Finally after what seemed like a long night, the banging stopped. Our father, passed out earlier, slept off the beer and as light filtered through the canvas, our mother gave us permission to get up. With caution and curiosity, we were all amazed to wake up to a "bear trap" with a real, live bear inside.

Again, Thank God for Park Wardens! The park wardens had quite a busy, risky night and now all were safe, at least for now.

Yes, that little, two-bed tent-trailer really was a wealth of many camping stories and I was grateful to survive them all.

Chapter 9

Turning thirteen is supposed to be a special birthday for kids and it certainly was for me. My Aunt Olivia decided to give me a beautiful, round, white transistor radio, which after 50-some years, is still owned and treasured by myself. Another, very dear aunt gave me a unique, pink step-ladder earring holder which was beautiful. To be loved on this special occasion by my Aunts, meant volumes, then and now, throughout my life.

Receiving a gift, of any kind, was almost never. At Christmas, when I was about nine years old, I was the receiver, of what seemed to me, a crushing, cruel act. I, unknowingly, was the butt of a so called joke, played on me by my mother. Since gift's were indeed rare and few, I was extremely excited about Christmas only to be humiliated and emotional knocked over while my self-esteem took a bashing. Christmas Eve came, supper eaten, now it was time for presents. It was my turn to un-wrap my few gifts. After eagerly waiting and anticipating the wrapped packages, I was totally dumbfounded and speechless, when inside a particular, nicely "bowed" package was a pile of Sparky's poop.

Together, the family laughed! Big laugh was had by all, that is, except me. I somehow failed to see the humor in it, at least for that time being. I wasn't sure how parents could be that cruel to their very own offspring or care so little of their child's feelings. However, over time, I forgave them and tried to see the humor. I somehow knew it was out of their own daily pain and poverty that they needed some sort of relief by a good laugh.

Chapter 10

$\mathcal{A}$ treasured, and close to my heart, vacation stood out, for me, like no other. At the age of 9 years old, my one aunt decided to donate money and send me to "church camp", if I wanted to go. This wonderful gift was from the same aunt that gave me the beautiful, white, round transistor radio for my thirteenth birthday. I was only jumping inside and out, by such an offer and so said "yes" with great expectations! Thanks mom and dad for letting me go!

This was going to be the only, one of two, times in my life that I was away from my family for a week. My Grandmother was one of the cook's for this little Pentecostal Church Camp and I was thrilled when I was able to sleep with Grandma in her little bunk room off the kitchen. Wow!

I was surrounded by loads of kid's, lot's of yummy food, exiting crafts and activities like hiking and swimming. There was also church time in a beautiful little camp chapel where lot's of preaching, singing and ministering went on in the evening. Then after Chapel was a great nighttime outing around the bonfire with tasty marshmallows and warm milk. Last but not least, there was Grandma's special, unending love from beginning to end. Nothing seemed as wonderful as all of this!

During that week, I asked Jesus into my heart and yes, I certainly felt and saw His Loving presence all around me. My convictions in Him were strong and later in my life, those same beliefs, brought me back from death's door. Thank you, precious Jesus, for saving my life over and over again.

Chapter 11

In my early teenage years while attending junior high school which was roughly ten blocks from our home, mom was still fighting MS and was doing the best for Jonathan and me as she possibly could.

Every school day I would walk each way, to and from our home and back equaling four mile's a day. That way I was kept in pretty good physical form. I wasn't in sports but I certainly "walked" a lot.

For lunch, at home, I usually got a nice hot baked potato with little else. Variety of food just wasn't in our home very often. Dad was the only one with a pay-check and he mostly bought cigarettes and booze. Mom was more and more house bound and yet she would make a grocery list, as best she could, and send it with dad. I don't believe my mother ever walked the grocery store isles while Jonathon and I attended school, but always tried desperately to have some food on hand for us two, hungry, growing kids.

In the winter time, mom made the best hamburger stew I ever tasted. And in the summer time, we were the recipients of our all time favorite, jelly powder and pudding. With these few luxuries, mom tried to make our lives as "normal" as possible, bless her trying heart.

As one summer day was unfolding, I was dealing with a heavy heart, so decided to approach my father, who was doing something in the garage. Now I don't know what I expected, but I asked anyways. At nine years old, I wanted so much to be able to buy small gifts for my mom's and dad's birthdays, so I came up to my dad and blurted the question out. "May I have ten cents a week for allowance?" I didn't even have a chance to say why, when my inquiring was squashed with a loud and definite "NO" and "Don't ask me again!" answer.

Poverty was thick in our lives and the drinking, smoking and MS kept us firmly planted in a no win situation for, which, took its ugly toll.

Chapter 12

After church camp there were many trials for me and my baby brother. I remember, after hours of my parents fighting, my dad thrashing around the house like a drunken sailor and my mom crawling on all fours from room to room, because she couldn't walk, and not so good memories of my own mental state.

I had gone to bed despite the ruckus and turmoil only to experience a sudden attack of anxiety, which I believe, now, was almost a nervous breakdown. At ten years old, tears uncontrollable, I staggered into the kitchen, way after dark, grabbed a utensil from the drawer and began bending it in half. Crying and sobbing, I didn't know which way to turn. The anguish and emotional pain was tearing my little head and heart in threads! Panic, hopelessness and fear rattled my entire being! God help me! Please Jesus, help me through this!

My emotionally strong yet physically broken mother heard me whaling, crawled to me on her hands and knees and told me firmly, "Elizabeth, go to bed!" The only thing

I could do was, to do just that. I threw the fork across the room and took my sorry self back, sobbing uncontrollably, to the bed I had come from. My mom could actually do nothing physically for me but her emotional strength somehow transferred to me, that horrible late night. Thank-you Mom, for trying to help me.

Dad, in his passed out state, was oblivious to any or all that was going on around him with his so called family.

As I look back now, I am totally grateful, that my father never critically physically harmed me. It came close and many times accusations were emotionally crippling and scarring, but never outwardly visible. At the age of thirteen or so my dad, again acting like Jeckle and Hide, almost broke both of my elbows completely backwards in half. He was standing, drunk, yelling at me, in-front of me, with both of my arms pulled straight forward. From underneath he applied tremendous pressure up against both outstretched elbows pushing them upwards, almost snapping them at the joint. God Forbid! Jesus Help Me! It was as if I was standing in the grip of Satin, Himself! I know, somehow, calling on the name of Jesus, Jesus intervened and Satin couldn't complete his crippling invasion on me!

None the less, emotionally I was scarred with yet another horrific experience and now had painful elbows to go with it. I was unable to straighten them for years after the attack. Again, thank you, my precious, Jesus for saving me, from permanent physical damage, when there was no one else!

Poverty stricken with emotional and physical illness

hanging thickly, weekend after weekend, within our home, mom crawled more and more. Kitchen to living-room, living-room to bathroom and back again, her knees became two large, round, thick "hoof like" calluses.

One thing mom always made sure to do, when my friend's were over, was to stay put wherever she was sitting, until they left. Mom had stopped seeing doctors and was on no medication at all and thank God, Mom wasn't in pain either. She just became more and more paralyzed from the waist down. With her arms she was strong enough to open jars and to lift herself up.

Again, as our existence was, sometimes, like that as the pit of Hell, my mother held her emotions inside. Even now, I am a bit angry at her silence or denial. She was very strong but I just don't get it, I guess I'm not that strong, and her inner strength was.

For years after my dad's death, my mother held severe bitterness inside and finally, after his dying day, stated on occasion some verbal anger towards him. Even then her lips were mostly sealed. A very popular quote of my mother was "If you have nothing nice to say, than don't say anything at all". Yes, she lived by her motto, perhaps by her faith, to the end of her seventy-six aching years.

Chapter 13

Now as the years unfolded, I became interested in boys, turned 16 and also started a part-time job at the south-end neighbor-hood, A & W. I took pride in being a "Car Hop" not a waitress and enjoyed my first official paying position for six months, ending the fall of 1973.

With my very first paycheck I took great pride in buying a new winter coat. I had never before had a "new Sears" catalogue coat. When it came, wild horses couldn't have got that garment off of my back, even if they ran me over. You see, for all my young years at home, I was probably one of the very first trend setters of buying strangers second hand clothing. Mom always listened to a radio program called "Swap Shop" every weekday morning. I remember my parents and me driving to different addresses around town to look at peoples boxed second hand clothes. New clothes just were not an option. Some of the houses we visited smelled and looked like someone or something had recently died within. Now, go figure, in this day and age, "second hand" stores are multi-million dollar businesses, selling almost anything you could possibly want to buy, in next to new condition. Quite an amazing turn around, I think!

As the next couple of years slowly passed by, my whole life took yet another serious turn for anxiety and emotional turmoil.

Somehow, my zeal for God, Jesus and the Holy Spirit, was forgotten through the daily pressures. The daily situations just seemed normal and ongoing year after year. As the situations just kept getting worse for our family, one thing did change. I was getting old enough to date boys and from 15 to 17 years old, I did have a couple of callers.

First there was a young hippy, wild kind, big hair boy whose name was "Mo Jo".

Well, I started seeing "Mo Jo" and felt he treated me quite nicely. Finally after about a month of so-called dating him, I took "Mo Jo" home to meet Mom.

During our three-some, ten minute visit, Mom kept her cool when we were face to face, but wow, after "Mo Jo" left, my soft spoken, not opinionated Mother, had a short but demanding talk with me. She did the talking and minced no words. "That boy is bad, bad news! Don't you ever go out with him again! My mom said she knew his family and never wanted any association between him and me again!

When my mom spoke so strongly, I just knew I had better listen! I trusted my mom. I cut off our relationship and never again saw that young man. To this day, I really don't know if he was bad or good, but I am grateful that my mom took the time to give me advice. Mom, I give you a sweet thank-you.

Chapter 14

By the time I was 17 years old, I had an engagement ring on my finger by another young man. It turned out to be one of the biggest mistakes I have made on my own. At eighteen and one half years of age I tied the marriage knot and jumped from the frying pan into yet another fire!

The man I was to marry was of a larger, rounder stature and he looked a lot like a younger version of my own father. Mom and dad both seemed to like this young man, perhaps because he came from a family with money, and both my parents and I thought, that in reality, that may make my life better.

Murrey was his name and for the two years before we wed, Murrey was in hot pursuit of me. Even during these two years of constant badgering from him, I knew I wasn't attracted to him, any way, shape or form. He was to me, obese and old, but was, indeed, very focused on what he wanted, which was me.

My little brother, six years younger than me, had his

own struggles after my wedding. Just one or two years before our mother died, she told me of Jonathan's emotional turmoil of when I got married and left home. For months after I left at eighteen, Jonathan was unable to eat or keep food down. Mom believed it was because he was suffering from the anxiety of being left alone in such a negative atmosphere. Again, a horrible "Flying Monkey"! God and Jonathan, please forgive me!

I had no idea my so called "escape" would be so hard on the very one that I loved. I had no clue, no idea what extra stress I was laying on a tender 12 year old. I wasn't aware of the internal anguish my baby brother faced. How stupid of me! He never told me and I was too busy trying to escape myself. Never once while Murrey was trying to sweep me off my feet, did I think to ask Jesus to lead me and show me the way.

I only looked at the obvious not the underlying motive. Cruelty was all around me. Before Murrey and I were married, there was an occasion, when, in my back yard, Murrey tickled Jonathan so intensely that Jonathan was forced to vomit. I had put Jesus aside and took my future in my own hands and now my family was paying for it.

While Murrey was in hot pursuit of me, I came to see his persistence as possibly love. Could he love me so much, he only really, wanted me? Every time I turned around, there Murrey was. Every place I wanted to go, Murrey wanted to take me there. I remember, with six years difference between us, he always seemed to know what he wanted and how to get it.

This takes me to the very first outburst of "controlling"

behavior that Murrey outwardly directed to me. Driving one day in his car, we were having a disagreement.

While Murrey was yelling at me, I threatened to get out of the car, while stopped at a stop sign. After my remark of possibly leaving, a huge enforcing voice proceeded to let me know that "If you get out of this car, you will never see me again!!" At seventeen with so little else good possibilities in my life, I became for the first time, totally controlled by another person, other than my parents. This man was going to be the father of my children and the control and lack of compassion was by no means going to get any better. You see, I stayed in the car and emotionally gave up any so called "rights" that at 18 were supposed to come with legal age.

At 17 ½, I was robbed of any so called opinions I may or may not have and for 13 ½ years, I tried to act like nothing was wrong. Over those, mostly loveless, years I was slowly dying while being eaten slowly with bitterness and loneliness.

I was bought by other people's money and so called prestige and dearly paid the "piper" by doing so. Just months before the August wedding date, it was time to pick the wedding parties colors. Now at 17, I didn't even know how to love myself let alone know how to stand up for myself.

Murrey and I had agreed on most of the arrangements but unfortunately we had quite a clash verbally about our choice of colors for the wedding party. For some reason, unknown to me, I definitely wanted the colors, green dresses for the women and brown jackets for the men. In no way possible did I want pink dresses and blue jackets. However, Murrey had his heart set on pink and blue. Well that turned out to be the second "huge" verbal blast that was intended for my ears. The uproar that came from the depth of his belly, I am sure, was heard, clearly, a block away.

This time his belly roar didn't sway my intentions. I told him frankly that I would walk out of the wedding totally if he tried to control the very essence of my special day. He demanded and won his way with me in the car at the stop sign, but that day, in early spring, I dug my heels in. I was determined that he was not going to intimidate me on this one!

You see when we were forcibly making color choices, the invitations were already mailed out and he didn't want to upset his parents by embarrassing them with me calling the wedding off.

We had a quest list of 200 people and most of them were his parent's friends. Little did I know the control was not to end with green dresses and brown jacket's. He dug his heels in and from that moment on Murrey did whatever Murrey wanted.

Chapter 15

Only after Murrey was successful in harnessing my life to his the amazing persistence and pursuing came to an abrupt end. After the marriage date, he no longer wanted my attention or conversation with me. He basically dropped me like a heavy rock. Now I believe, the one only reason he wanted me so much was because, I did not want him. In his mind, I was some kind of contest trophy. After approximately two years of chasing me, he was then able to set his accomplishments or trophy, me, Elizabeth, on the mantle.

On the night of our honeymoon, I was very hurtfully put in my place by the very man I married.

As Murrey lay on the bed of our apartment, he watched me as I very shyly took off my clothing. I was just 18 years old and had never undressed in front of any man. As I stood there naked, facing the open door closet, my new obese husband told me matter-of-factly, "You sure do have a saggy bum." I was 5'8", 18 years old and weighed 120 pounds, soaking wet. At that time of my life, I didn't feel like I was in any way over-weight. And now my husband, of only hours old, was criticizing and putting me down. I didn't know how to respond or what to say or do. I only felt the deep cutting pain of rejection unleashed on me. Betrayal and control were essence of the night.

Chapter 16

The first two years passed mostly uneventful. There were still occasion to fight for myself but it took the form of things like wanting to buy a broom for the kitchen and bathroom linoleum.

For six months before our wedding, I had been working fulltime, as work experience through school, at an accounting office as the receptionist, secretary. After grade 12 school graduation, the company hired me on full-time. Still, it took another huge blow up between Murrey and me, for me to get permission to buy a broom. At this very moment, it seems totally impossible for such an argument to have taken place, for anyone, but, unfortunately I guess, he liked me under his thumb with control.

He stated that his mom never owned a broom therefore I also was to do without one. Was this, just a little controlling and narrow minded? Perhaps, yes. I think so.

Months before we were married, I started studying for my driver's license. I was excited and asked Murrey to assist me with the project. First he said for me to wait until after our wedding, so I studied and waited. Well, like everything else important to me, Murrey tried to put a stop to me driving, also. After we came back from our honeymoon, I was informed, "My mom doesn't drive, so you don't need to either!

Again I was in another fight for my very existence and independence. I made up my mind and made an appointment for driving education lessons, for after work hours. I walked to and from them and also paid the bill. There was no moral or emotional support from the man I married, let alone love. Basically, I knew I was on my own, but it wouldn't be that bad would it?

The disappointment, control and lack of love, just didn't stop. I remember coming home to Murrey's parent's home only about a year after we were married, to find him busily absorbed into a "porn" magazine for men. For some reason, I was again somewhat naive about such things, because I thought when you're a newlywed, spouses were happy with each others bodies. Growing and exploring each other bodies couldn't possibly become "old news" already? Could it?

I grabbed the magazine from his hands while he was drooling over the pictures of naked women, with in. While screaming at him in shock, I threw the horrible magazine out into the backyard.

Looking back at that time of our lives, me at 19 and him at 25, were both so unhappy but yet we didn't have the courage or faith to change anything.

Chapter 17

As time passed by, I felt paternal instincts kicking in. I wanted a baby. Murrey, at 26, was still not ready. I don't think he was willing to give up his special status with his mom and dad, just yet. Now Murrey was used to being the only child and, with that, he was very accustomed to having just about anything he wanted. Little did I know it, but us having a child, was about to change our whole life.

God knows everything and His Holy Word says He is very patient. I was not living my life as a dedicated believer, but I believe God, Himself, knew how to bring me back into the flock.

Sometime in May of 1978, I received the wonderful news of "us" being pregnant! I was going to have a baby! I had worked at the accounting firm for three years and now I was about to enter "mother-hood". On learning of the special news, we wanted to share this tidbit with our parents.

My mom and dad were excited for us but their reaction wasn't quite the same for Murrey's mother. We went to her office at a department store and proceeded to share the good news. However, after telling her, the first thing out of her mouth was, "I'm not old enough to be a grandma!" Ouch! I felt like I had just stepped on her toes.

Gratefully, however, after the initial shock, all seemed to be "OK". Little did I know it, but this was the start of a bit of a wonderful whirlwind within our daily routine.

Within literally weeks, after our baby news, Murrey and I started looking for a house for our offspring and us. We had saved some money during the past three years and now it was time to buy a house! First we were shown already built homes in older areas of the city and as one house lead to another, we also viewed new homes in the new areas. Wow, until now, I had never experienced such adventure! What an awesome experience that was!

Being pregnant triggered, for the first time in my 20 years of life, an opportunity to have my first child, build a new home and hopefully many more positive situations. I truly thought that our marriage may become strong though all of this. I knew I was certainly being swept off my feet with goodness and excitement!

After surveying the housing situation, within the community, we happily decided to build our dream home. A few years earlier, like in 1975, many first time life changing situations occurred in my life like graduation and marriage. But it seemed 1978 was even bigger. A new baby, a brand new home, a new car, new furniture and even a small vacation to B.C., while pregnant, were exciting and breathtaking to behold.

Nothing could impose its ugliness or cruelty to hurt me emotionally, at this wonderful time of life, or could it?

As our house was being finished, inside and out, my new in-law's decided to give Murrey and me a special house warming gift. We really appreciated the generous intentions because the gift was to be "front room furniture". However, there was only one stipulation, they picked it out. Now I am not ungrateful for the furniture, but somehow, I felt, very, cheated out of my own independence. I was an adult, working, pregnant, married, and yet, treated as if I didn't even exist. Before the furniture was bought, I went to my husband and protested the whole idea, with tears and anxiety. I told Murrey we could save up for our own furniture, but, again, my words fell on deaf ears.

I cried and told Murrey how offended I was, but again, my wishes and dignity, was ignored. Again, in the middle of all the excitement, I relinquished my very rights in the face of Murrey and his parent's subtle "control".

As I look back, I see myself as wanting to be spoiled with "stuff", but actually in the process I was giving up my own mind of likes, dislikes, right and wrong, choices. Instead of growing and developing daily, I was being chipped away at and becoming less and less of a responsible adult. For the sake of "having things" I was abandoning my very self worth and dignity.

Chapter 18

In the middle of house construction, we set off for Penticton, B.C. It's amazingly funny how disrespect and ugliness have a way to attack the very giver of such. Always be aware of "flying monkey's".

We booked a very nice hotel with a restaurant by the beach. Again, I was six months pregnant, not showing to much with my first child and Murrey still didn't show much warm feelings for me. It was so obvious to me, as I sat on the beach in shorts and a t-shirt, while Murrey in his swimming trunks, took to his air mattress and waded out into deeper waters.

There he clung onto a vertical steel pole planted out in the middle of the beach water cove. There as he lay on his stomach, he was mesmerized, while watching women, of all ages in skimpy bikinis. Not once did he come in to see if I was ok or hungry or perhaps lonely. After hours and hours of sitting by myself, with no one to talk to and the sun was going down and Murrey decided he had viewed enough, for that day.

I guess God thought it was time for a "dancing chicken". Not once did Murrey consider the strength of the sun. That night, in a very nice room, Murrey paid the "piper". His back and legs were burnt so badly it was almost critical. No amount of lotion cooled the burning, bright red skin over most of his body.

While Murrey suffered with moans and groans throughout the night, I had a rather wonderful sleep. The next day we tenderly headed for home.

On the way back we went through Cranbrook, B.C., where I was to meet yet another "flying monkey".

On our travels home we stopped at Cranbrook. Now at six months pregnant, I had no idea what I was in for. Cranbrook to our home city is about a 4 ½ hour drive straight through and that is exactly what we did. Not once was the car stopped for a bathroom break. God help me! By the time we reached home my stomach hurt so badly I could hardly get out of the car on arrival. As I look at it now, I really should have peed right then and there, in Murrey's wonderful car.

Murrey wanted to see how fast his new car would do the distance and I think the red, painful skin was getting to him also, there-fore we didn't stop.

Looking back now, it doesn't even seem real, but it was!

Chapter 19

As 1978 was coming to an end, my tummy was growing right on target. It seemed that after I quit my accounting position, there was a lot of free time for me. Murrey had always gone to the Medicine Hat Tiger hockey games and that still was happening. I couldn't sit nor wanted to sit through game after game. Since I didn't like hockey violence, I spent a lot of evenings at home by myself. I didn't see Murrey during the daytime, as he was at work, and the hockey arena was his evening hangout.

However, as I approached nine months pregnant, I also had my hospital suitcase packed. My patience was running a little thin with Murrey always coming home from a hockey game in the wee early hours of the next morning. The hockey games were over by 10:30 p.m. and only God knows, for sure, where he went until 7:00 a.m. the next day, on numerous occasions.

Finally very tired of the emotional abuse, I took the situation into my own hands.

Early, one morning, around 3:00 a.m., Murrey still

wasn't home and as usual, I couldn't sleep or relax by myself. I got out of bed, nine months pregnant, got dressed, picked up my suitcase and went to my car. There I stacked the suitcase in the back seat and got into the drivers seat.

After starting the car, now in the middle of winter, I drove down the street about ½ a block and turned onto the Crescent. There I parallel parked the car about five houses down the crescent, turned off the lights, and proceeded to wait for the man of the morning.

I don't know for sure how long I waited, but after a couple of hours or so, I saw Murrey driving his truck past the crescent entry road, slowly and certainly in no rush to go home.

Sitting in the dark, again, I waited. In less than five minutes, Murrey in his truck, flashed past the crescent entrance down our home street, in quite a hurry! Because I was not in bed at home, my suitcase gone, Murrey was under the opinion that I had driven myself to the hospital, possibly having his baby.

Mission impossible was successful! My very inconsiderate, self-centered husband was sent on a wild goose chase. After seeing him speed away from the house, I turned on the vehicle and proceeded back to my warm bed, in my warm house.

Later that morning, Murrey came back home, disgusted and angry. Yes, I sure did get a tongue lashing and I knew it wasn't the last fallout between us, but I really couldn't help myself. I had to fight back, somehow.

Chapter 20

On December 14, 1978, was the mark, of the start, of more "dancing chickens" or miracles that eventually would become welcomed daily within my life. Also on December 14, 1978, I delivered a very beautiful baby boy, Mackenzie Alexander. Big Blue eyes and an adorable little face were truly a mother's delight.

It seemed this was the moment in time that God, the Father, started calling me back to His Truth.

Mackenzie was calm, smiling, happy, content and growing. Within weeks of his birth, we started planning his baptism. That is also when, as an unbaptised adult, I was yearning also to be baptized. My younger brother and I, for some reason, had never been baptized in our lives. Perhaps it was because of my Grandmother's Pentacostle upbringing or perhaps the very dysfunctional environment within our home. In the Pentacostle church, young children were verbally "blessed" by the pastor and then as an adult, to confirm their faith in Jesus, they would be "dunked" or baptized into a body of water. I don't know for sure why my brother and I weren't, but now with my very first child, that opportunity certainly was here.

There was no doubt in my mind that Jesus is the Son of God and it was time I had a public religious ritual to confirm my belief of this. How special could this be? My baby, and me, having a baptismal service together. From the very core of my being this felt so very right.

A day before the service, which was held at the United Church, I was visited by the Holy Spirit, while having a nap on the couch. Mackenzie Alexander was in his crib sleeping peacefully and I on the couch when, in my sleep, my soul sat up and saw through the bedroom wall. It was as if I was having an out of body experience. As my body slept, my soul saw a Great Wind blowing into our bedroom window from outside, as the burgundy curtains flew horizontally upwards, inside the room, instead of just hanging there. The Great Wind was strong and fast. Then I heard the wind gusts coming down the house hallway. Just before the Great Wind reached me, I woke up! There was no more sign of a wind sound or sight. It was just gone.

At that moment of waking up, I knew I had just witnessed my first encounter with the Holy Spirit. I learned later that God's word, the Holy Bible, calls the Holy Spirit the Great Wind.

The next day, Mackenzie and I, were both sprinkled, and baptized in the name of the Father, Son, and Holy Spirit. Thank you, Father for your Holy Trinity Presence.

I didn't know it yet, but this new spiritual awakening was a new spiritual journey just waiting to unfold.

Chapter 21

Our little Mackenzie truly was one of life's best blessings so far. He was a perfect baby. He was content, he was beautiful, he was playful and he was my offspring, my blood and wonderful gift from God. For almost two years I was totally on cloud nine. Then Murrey and I decided to have another child. How exciting! Baby number two, for us. This time I was due on Labour Day, September 7. Mackenzie was due November 30, but chose to wait another two weeks, to the day to be born. Mackenzie was my very best ever Christmas gift and now baby #2 was going to be my summer time gift from God.

Before Kirby Erick came on the scene, there was much work to do on the new home front. For those early childhood days of Mackenzie and Kirby's, I was elected to be main bottle washer, house cleaner, weed puller, potatoes planter, laundry personal, chief cook, house doctor, dish washer and anything else that was needed around the home front. I worked hard but was extremely happy that I could stay home with my precious babies.

The house finances were never talked about and I was kept totally in the dark concerning our financial picture. Murrey didn't seem too interested in kids stuff, so for Mackenzie, Kirby and I, much of our time was spent just the three of us.

Now going back, to the early summer of 1981, just before Kirby's birth, our house was finished but our back yard needed three feet of top soil. The summer before, we put top soil down in the front yard and planted potatoes. However, now two and a half years later while I was eight months pregnant our back yard still needed three huge piles of topsoil. With hardly any communication between husband and wife, I decided I would have to try, by hand, to level as much of it as possible.

I really, to this day, do not know what Murrey's intentions were for those piles of dirt, because as evening after evening, in the hot sun, eight months pregnant and me shoveling dirt, Murrey would lay on his favorite chair and watch sports on T.V.

Finally after many hot days and evenings, the top soil was leveled. However, I at eight months pregnant was only able to make a small dent in the huge piles. About two weeks after I attempted moving the dirt, Murrey hired a manned small tractor to do the leveling. Finally, our back yard became the proper soil level, and thank God, Himself, that I didn't have a miscarriage in the process.

Two weeks before Labour Day, we had a wonderful surprise of events. August 28, 1981, Kirby Erick came to live in our home as our second beautiful son! Mackenzie had been exactly two weeks late while Kirby was exactly two weeks early.

Approximately two months before Kirby was born, Murrey and I were watching an old western movie. In this movie was a family of brothers that were all distinctive and honorable men. The one brother especially was tall, dark, handsome, honest and a sheriff. The actor that played that character was actually "Tom Selleck" whom at that time was, I thought, awesome.

As we sat watching the actors portray such charm, Murrey and I discussed the possibility of naming our second child, if born a boy, the name of "Tom Seleck's" character, "Kirby".

Like I said earlier, August 28, 1981, Kirby Erick, was born. Thank you Father God! The name of our new son was, at that time, quite a new name in society, and I was a bit nervous at first, but felt very compelled that the name Kirby Erick was definitely the exact, right name for our precious, new beautiful, baby boy.

For approximately a year and a half after Kirby was born, my precious little boy cried and cried. Every night, for that year and a half, I would sit in the rocking chair for hours on end in the living room, holding and rocking my very upset little boy.

When Kirby was four months old, he too was baptized. He cried before and after church, but for the entire church service, my sweet baby, slept cradled in my arms. By the Grace of God, my precious crying baby was content and peaceful for the whole church service. Glory to God! Thank you for blessing my child!

As Mackenzie and Kirby grew, they were always a huge joy in my life. They would play for literally hours on end. As I would be doing the inside house chores, my two beautiful boys, would be underfoot. When I would be doing dishes, they played between my feet. When I went to make the beds, they followed within a foot's distance. When it came time to have their baths, I gave them lots of bubbles to dive through and pop. We were never apart!

At that time of my life, our home was usually messy but, as always, I claim, messy is different than dirty.

As Mackenzie and Kirby were only 4 and 2, my closeness with Murrey was almost never. We ate our meals in different rooms, the kids and I in the kitchen around the kitchen table and he in the living room, in front of the TV set.

Actually, Murrey had very little to do with his children and me. I had my two beautiful boys love but I needed to be loved by a best friend, husband. I had no one to talk to or share my thoughts with. Inside, a part of me was dyeing cell by cell, day after day. I kept focused, as best I could, in my small world, for I knew my children needed me more than they would ever know, and I them.

Chapter 22

In the summer of 1984, the boys were growing and were always playfully running around. For adventures, Mackenzie, Kirby and I would spend endless time in the yard, at the playground parks, go swimming, bike and take Abby, our dog, for walks.

One summer day that stands out vividly in my mind, was a certain trip to Echo Dale Park. On this particular Saturday the crowd was thick. The park that day was having some special events and it seemed like everyone from our fair city was there.

With Mackenzie, holding on to one hand and Kirby holding onto the other, we set off through the maze of people, with our towels, blanket and food. Not once did I realize the danger we were in. To be in such a large crowd, with two little boys, was about to take a serious turn for the worse.

People's shoulders were almost touching while circulating around the beach and lake area.

One minute, as the three of us walked, every thing was

fine. The very next moment, fear and panic raced through me like lightning. My Kirby, two years old, tiny baby boy was gone! Gone? How could that be?! How could I not have seen or felt him go?! He was holding my hand!

I frantically searched, while clutching and gripping Mackenzie's little hand. My baby Kirby, Oh God, please bring back my baby! Trying to control shear terror within my soul, while darting through the sea of people, I prayed. There were tears of fear welling up inside me, while trying not to lose and scare my little Mackenzie. Not feeling the time lapse, anguish seemed to smoother my very breathing.

All of a sudden, only Jesus knows for sure how long after Kirby was missing, a loud voice came over the intercom air waves.

The man's voice announced that a little boy had been found and could the parent's please come to the office to pick him up!

Praise God! My Jesus kept my baby safe! Truly miracles are real and I thank God for each and every one!

Mackenzie and I raced, zigg-zagging through the twisted path of people. On approaching the office, I saw Kirby. I don't remember anything except me picking him up and the lifeguard telling me vaguely that an older gentleman had found Kirby and brought him to the lost and found booth.

I couldn't believe my emotions. First, when I picked up my tiny, little boy, I held inside of me horrible anger that I have never felt before, in my whole life. At that very second, red hot anger engulfed my every fiber. How could I have misplaced him?! I held him very tightly, tighter than ever before and hugged him as we made our way back to the car. Gripping tightly onto Mackenzie's fragile hand, I hugged Kirby's little body to my chest while slowly as we walked, much needed, pure sweet relief washed over my entire body. I knew in my mind, body and heart that Jesus is alive and protects his very own. All I can say is thank you, Jesus with my hearts sincere gratitude.

Chapter 23

Little did I know it yet, but my life and that of my children, was about to change dramatically in the next few years.

Murrey still was, as always, uninterested in me and our children, but was along for the ride, at least for awhile. One thing I did faithfully was to read a little of my bible's verses on a regular basis after my baptism, which lead me to leave the United Church a year and a half later.

Instinctively I decided to go to my Grandmother's Pentacostal church for their services. After attending for couple of months I asked Jesus into my broken, almost love empty life. My two beautiful boys were the only source of strength I had. My mother, Gertie, was unable to carry my loneliness and deprived state, while my father was fighting his own liquor battles. He had just been laid off of his truck driving job and found he had no money except what Mom gave him. Mom, on AISH, had become the wage earner and provider in their meager state.

They loved me, but I was in this marriage by my self.

First Murrey and his mother were inseparable and then after her death, Murrey and his father were inseparable. My father-in-law, at that time, when I was fighting for my very existence, relayed to me that Murrey's mother died because of me. Apparently, I broke her heart. I was suffering in silence with no husbandly love and then, wow, I was attacked again! That family really stuck together.

Chapter 24

In June of 1985, I hit rock bottom. I in my mental state of loveless, cold controlling emotional abuse could take no more. For the last eleven years of marriage, I had always focused my attentions to something, anything else, besides marriage loneliness and my broken heart. As a young mom, I had continued going to church and also took up physical exercises, such as swimming and aerobics. I had always had an inner need to be loved, to succeed in life and to grow old.

After my children and I were baptized, we attended the Pentacostal Church. As life started changing drastically, I continued to read God's Holy Word, "The Bible". For some reason, I understood a lot of the content within. I found that as I attended church with my two sons and kept reading the Bible, the Holy Spirit, was gently leading me into my future of total grace, love, happiness and a fulfillment in my life's journey that I had never yet experienced.

On the home front, life was hollow and void of caring. I loved my children and they loved me, but I needed a caring, loving husband to share my life and feelings. The more I got grounded in the Holy Living Word, the deeper the black despair lurked in our home.

The more I read, the more enlightened, and excited I became about God's Truth. And the more I grew in faith, the more my husband seemed to hate me and what I stood for. Murrey called "believing in God" a "crutch and it seemed as though Murrey hated the thought of not being in "control" of me. In his eyes, my new found relationship with Jesus only meant that I was somehow less of a person. What I was learning day by day, was that Jesus loves me so much, that He died a horrible death on the cross and rose three days later, so I could have life abundantly. Yes He claimed that was abundantly, not to just exist. His Holy Word was, as I read, brimming full of Holy Promises just waiting for any person, young or old, to claim for themselves. As I read page after page, beautiful, abundant promises jumped up into my head and heart, as I digested every paragraph.

Murrey only tolerated me before I became a Christian and now he could barely stand to be in the same house as me as a Christian.

As the emotional abuse was worsening, I ate less and less. I exercised to the extreme, every day of the week and put on a happy public face. People didn't see inside me but Jesus did. My body was actually disappearing in the mirror as I at 5'8" tall became a walking, talking skeleton. At my low peek, I weighed in at 117 lb. It became so bad that I actually lost the ability to eat any food and keep it down. I had lost the ability to eat. Again, the more I believed in

God, the more my husband hated me and God. The emotional blackmail and acute exercising brought me to the cross-roads of my entire young life.

Chapter 25

It was June 1985 and the dam broke. All hell broke loose in my life to the point that it felt like my life was an enormous cyclone whirlwind being sucked into a bottomless drain. I can't even remember every ugly detail. All I knew was that I was fighting for the very breath in my body while praying, trusting and trying to manage such a sour marriage. I was, without a doubt, anorexic.

I admitted myself to hospital, only to find that the doctors there couldn't help me. I was terrified for my very life and I still couldn't eat. God in His Mercy then took the poisonous situation out of my hands and put my very body and life into professional stranger's expertise hands.

After a couple of days of no improvement and signs that I was going down, a last chance decision, by the doctor's, was made. I was quickly air lifted to a larger hospital where my fate would be decided. "To live or to die?" that was the question.

I still couldn't eat and my weight was still dropping. I didn't know it but, with one leg in the grave, Jesus still had a couple of miracles up His sleeve, after all, I was one of His new adopted children! Again, Jesus the Physician was present and delegating.

Within the first 24 hours of being at this new hospital, my very last breath was almost taken. The day after I got there, as I was walking down the cold white corridors, I instinctively experienced again that I absolutely do have a soul. Only moments before I received medication, a very disturbing situation arouse, that by the Grace of God passed, shortly after I ingested medication.

For a brief moment, while walking, I could not see out of my eye sockets. It seemed as though my "insides" or soul had made a right-hand turn, inside my body. I do believe my soul was painfully tearing up inside of me and making ready to go home to heaven, though death. The pain accumulated though out my life's journey had reached maximum overloading proportions and my young naive body, mind and soul could take absolutely no more!

Within a short time after taking the medication, my body reprogrammed properly and I was able to focus through my eyes again. This medication also brought with it the ability to ingest food and keep it down. For a week's period of time, on medication, I went through the regular routines of normal life, within the protected walls of the hospital and by the end of five full days, I had gained five pounds. Praise God, I was gaining some weight! Food was staying down and digesting! It looked like I was going to live! That "dancing chicken" I have never forgotten. Praise God Almighty!

At the end of the first week, I received a bus ticket from

the hospital, to go home for the weekend. There my Mom and Dad were waiting for me at the bus depot. For some reason, Murrey had better things to do, and I wasn't it. During this time, I learned he was planning to take our two little boys on a vacation, to a condominium at a resort in the USA. That was the first year he had ever been there and liked it so much, it became one of his high priority spots.

The weekend was 1 and a half days long, because Sunday, early afternoon, I was hitching a ride back to the hospital via one of Murrey's cousins and wife, in there motorhome. I had only received a weekend pass and was on my way back again, to my refuge hospital. This is when Murrey and our young children went to enjoy themselves in their getaway luxury condo, me in the hospital fighting for my very life and him relaxing, being spoiled, in contentment. It was as though he was actually celebrating my demise.

Somehow, that "flying monkey" was very large and hurt deeply in my shattered heart as I carried that emotional bruise for many years to come.

However, it looked like I was being given a second chance in life as I kept believing but not speaking my faith. I kept praying silently and trusting Jesus for something I certainly could not do on my own.

The second week of my stay in hospital, I had an aunt, uncle, and cousin come to visit me. They took me out for lunch and gave me their moral support. I felt so embarrassed, for being in such a bad way, I could hardly express myself of my gratefulness for their visit. They brought me clothing and sundries. I basically had not one person to shoulder the loneliness and inside pain and abandonment.

I silently cried out "God, please help me. I need You." I said "Nobody really loves me." God's word said, "I love you." John 3:1 I said, "I feel all alone." God's word said, "I will never leave you or forsake you." Hebrews 13:5 I cried out "I can't go on" God's word said, "My grace is sufficient" II Corinthians 12:9 I hung onto every promise I could remember in my short time of being a born again Christian. I said in my despair, "It's impossible", God said: "All things are possible" Luke 18:27.

Then on the Thursday of my second and final week's stay, I received moral support in the form of a letter from my cousin. In our adult lives, my cousin and I were not very close, but she had it in her heart enough to love me through this letter. God bless her heart for caring. She will probably never know how deeply important that correspondence was and how critical was the timing.

Finally Saturday came and I was on my second bus ride home. My dad had been sober for about a year by now and he said he would be at the bus depot to pick me up. Dad was there and again I went home to a negative, love empty dwelling.

Chapter 26

July 1985, finally arrived, only after a horrific June and life went on like nothing ever happened. I kept my faith to myself and went through the mother and wife role for the next three years. Every night Jesus was my last, in my head, silent, prayer of conversation. Every night I would lie there silently and talk for an hour to the very God that saved my life. Every night, rain or shine, I prayed for His Grace and Mercy to lead me and guide me, and protect me from further harm.

My children were growing and I was slowly healing from the inside out. I gained weight gradually and restored my mental and physical health through faith, medication and prayer.

I had worked my total body muscles so hard, by exercising, that they needed ample time and bed rest to heal and regain strength. The very first week of being home again, I took to the pavement to look for a part-time job. I pushed my weak and ragged body until I was hired at a local women's clothing store. There I was barely able to stand and work my three hour shifts. Right after the shifts worked I would retreat home in my car and pancake onto to the sofa, only to fall fast asleep.

The weeks passed slowly, but I kept fighting and striving for wellness, mind, body and soul. My marriage was not getting any better. There was no emotional support, love or caring. Jesus' love was real.

However, my feelings, towards my spouse, were turning to that of hatred and resentment for what I was experiencing in my own home. To my spouse, money was more important than anything from my heart. The importance of prestige, money, and material things was tearing me apart and I was starting to hate everything Murrey stood for.

Still as a fairly new born again Christian, I was hurtfully criticized by my husband, his family and his friends. I said nothing verbally to a single person. I catered to them and went through the motions as best I could without exploding.

I knew God was with me, because His precious word proclaimed "He would never leave me or forsake me." Hebrews 13:5 After all, my life was spared or, in my eyes, saved for eternity sake and for this life's sake.

First the Holy Spirit came to visit me the day before Mackenzie's and my baptism and then again a few years later, before I received medication for my severe anorexic condition.

As daily prayer was my vehicle towards Heaven, I had a beautiful encounter again with the Holy Spirit. He visited me again during one night after months of sever stomach pain, before medication. I had a large open sore on my left knee that was open and bleeding for months. With my extreme anxiety before hospitalization, I came to think that with a non healing open sore and acute stomach problems, that perhaps I also had the C word, Cancer.

However, again late into the night, I had crawled into bed with Mackenzie and Kirby because I wasn't wanted in my own bed.

As I was laying there, I heard again the sound of rushing wind, blowing within the house hallway. As soon as it became quite loud, I sat up-right, Kirby in his crib and Mackenzie beside me, on his bed. Within seconds of sitting up, the Great Wind came through the door of Mackenzie's bedroom and my chest was penetrated by the most incredible love force I have ever, ever experienced!

The instant the Wind entered my chest I immediately slowly started to lay back down from shear ecstasy while my chest and stomach felt like beautiful rainbow love fireworks exploding within me. It was a bit like electricity but the presence of unbelievable, undeniable love was so pure and gentle, that, moments later, I fell fast asleep.

The next morning my stomach pained no more and the open sore, on my left knee that was bleeding for at least two continuous months, had dried up and new skin had been placed over it. There was however a slight mark of different color where the sore had been, but with my new pain free stomach and leg, I knew with out a doubt, that the Holy Spirit, the night before, had totally healed my body from something very serious, as I had been the recipient of an encounter with our Almighty God, Himself.

Praise the Lord, for His Mercy is for all. At that very

moment I asked the Lord to never erase the spot on my knee, for I never, ever wanted to forget one of the most beautiful, important things Jesus has ever done for me. Little did I know it, but God had taken over my situation through prayer and with my growing faith, miracles and "dancing chicken's" were transpiring right before my eyes.

Again, I can't express the total appreciation I held and hold deep within my very core for the very Jesus that saved me over and over again. I had not one single person to help me shoulder the crazy, inhuman abuse, and with me turning acutely towards God through petitioning prayer, Jesus saw that and stepped in to carry me through the black storm. Thank you, Father for your precious Son.

My knee was healed and my stomach wasn't in pain but about two and one half months later, I still admitted myself to hospital because I could not ingest food and keep it down. God had more work planned for my bodies benefit, this time by professional doctor's hands.

Chapter 27

After the hospitalization and medication for the anorexic condition, I tried, for almost three years, to mend and continue to bring some kind of love into my marriage. All the while, every night, I would talk secretly to my Savior, Jesus. As I prayed continually, by the night time hours, I grew and healed more and more inside. My soul that had been also anorexic was beginning to become healthier and stronger with ever year. I prayed for my husband, our children, our friends, and our families. I continued to pray for guidance, strength and help and also to thank God for His very existence.

Almost three whole years passed and the anguish building up inside me from the constant emotional abuse, lack of love and constant ridicule from my husband caused an enormous change in our family lives.

With three years of bending backwards emotionally, praying and hoping for positive change, there was none to be seen in our home. It seemed as though I was again boiling over within my heart and mind. It seemed I had no alternative, again.

So leading up to December 07, 1988, I had been looking for other living quarters through the news paper. I was desperate and I needed out! My father-in-law had recently told me that I was totally barking up the wrong tree. He told me, with his son beside him, that when people die, they go six feet down and it is all over. Finished, capoot, done for, the end! They kept trying to blackmail me emotionally for my very beliefs. They wanted me to be their servant and clone, God Forbid! Thank God for the medication. The turmoil was still not over.

Every supper hour and reaching long into the morning hours, Murrey would be content to watch television all by himself. He would come home from work, fill his plate and leave the kitchen. The boys and I ate regularly, around the kitchen table, for all of our meals. We liked each others company but I guess Murrey didn't.

Knowing, by experiencing, that Jesus had saved my mortal body, weak and broken and knowing God's word was alive in me by studying His precious Word, I trudged onward. Believing and again knowing beyond a doubt, my relationship with Jesus was what made the difference between living empty, dying or becoming strong, vibrant and truly loved. I continued to choose life.

God's Holy word reinforced in me that "God is the Rewarder of those that seek Him". Philippians 4:19 God's scripture told me, "That if any man, woman or child left mother, father, spouse or child for God's Sake, He would bless that person following Him a hundred fold". Again I trusted His word.

It spoke volumes to me because for three years, I desperately tried, unsuccessfully to repair this whole marriage mess. One thing I was learning was that it takes two hands to clap and it takes both marriage partners to make a successful relationship.

I felt that my children's eventual faith in God was at stake and if I continued to live a, total lye, I would probably die, only this time of hatred, bitterness and a broken heart.

Please God, forgive me for anger and resentment. "Help me Jesus", I continued to pray.

Chapter 28

Finally December 07, 1988 came. It was getting close to Christmas and total devastation, cruelty and dark abandonment was in every corner of our home. It was late at night, the boys were tucked into bed, Murrey watching television and I, empty, hurting, desperate, was lying in bed. With no evidence of any positive changes for our so called family, I was on my bed, knowing only God Himself could intervene.

In shear anguish, I resorted back to my prayer channel. I told God, while tears flooded my face and cry's for help, that I wanted to leave my husband. I cried because I was totally void of any material or personal ability to fend on my own, let alone with two little boy's. As I sat on my bed, with Murrey in the living-room, my cry's for God's help continued long into the night. I cried, prayed and cried, petitioning my Lord for help. My pleas were frantic. This went on for literally hours and hours, until, early a.m.

I fell asleep exhausted and drained of all anxiety. Shortly after falling asleep, early in the morning, God gave me another dream. God showed me as I was, in my dream, looking up at a very amazing sight. There in the sky was Jesus and a cloud made of His followers covering the sky with Him.

When I woke up I knew I had just witnessed Jesus' second coming, "The Rapture". I believe God had given me a glimpse into man-kinds future and definitely mine. I believe that I will see The Lord's second coming and I knew deep in my spirit, that Christ, Himself, was watching over me.

Thank you, awesome Creator and Physician! Yes the "dancing chicken's" were certainly appearing and my hopes were mounting!

Early that morning the door bell rang and there, outside were three women that were my friends that I never thought before, could help me. I let them in, while their posture and faces were that of steel, they proceeded to instruct me that I was not leaving my home without my two children.

Praise God, I got back-up! My husband left the pow-wow and God showed me that I had moral support. Things were moving so fast. I rented a small basement apartment but I was too distraught to stay there overnight. Therefore I moved back into our house, where Murrey was.

Chapter 29

On waking the next morning, while Mackenzie and Kirby were at school, I called a divorce lawyer and by the grace of God she saw me for a visit that afternoon. From her office, after telling her my story, she picked up the phone and dialed my employment manager. I had worked there fulltime for the last two and half years of my life. My new lawyer told my boss that a family crisis had taken place and I would not be available for work until further notice. I was then instructed to confirm this message to my boss on completion of the phone call. My lawyer then instructed me to go home, pack suite-cases for my children and my self, pick the boys up after school, at school, and proceed to the women's shelter.

God proceeded to put every professional support person necessary in my path for my way out of this undeniable hollow marriage.

On arrival of the women's shelter, my poor children were rattled with devastation, with such a drastic measure in their young lives. However, I really had no alternative and I knew I had to listen to the professional people sent to help me escape my mental abuser. I also did this move because I loved my boys so much! I wanted them to be free of the extreme control, false priorities and negativity. I felt deeply that all these new occurrences were lead by the hand of God and now I had to obey and trust Him.

It turned out that for two complete weeks we were confined to the Shelter and my boys were hurt deeply from the anxiety and the pain from being there and not at their own home. Kirby had a physical thrashing episode with one of the counselors while Mackenzie remained quiet, reserved, withdrawn because he was petrified.

After three years of being on medication, I had gained fifty pounds. I had gone from mere skeleton bones to 165 pounds and I knew that as a young mom, I was on the plump side and growing. But in the 14 days that we lived like prisoners at our refuge shelter, I was tense and almost numb from the unknown future and actions I was taking. I kept silently praying and thanking The Holy Trinity for prayers answered and for my children and our future needs.

The moment by moment stress and numbness caused my weight to literally melt from my very body, right before my eyes! In our two week stay, I shed 20 pounds. I know for a fact that extreme anxiety, fear and stress together stops and limits the proper digestion of food and nutrition. Food just passes right through on these occasions. Seeing my boys horror unfolding before me, being like a captive, not doing my employment, not knowing what God had in-store ahead and dealing with total fear and hatred of my estranged husband for pushing me emotionally this far was hurtful, to say the least, and tearing me up viciously inside. My children and I were scared for our very existence!

As our days at the shelter unfolded, I refused telephone calls from my estranged husband and for relief reasons I was instructed to write my feelings, in detail, on paper. If I wouldn't have released my turmoil, I don't know how I would have coped. The occurrence of a mental break down was something I did not want or need at this crippling time. Again, thank God for the medication prescribed three years earlier.

With my babies anger outbreaks of horror, we were crippled and deeply scarred emotionally only to find a small comfort in the presence of sincerely caring counselors. To keep busy, the kids had a counselor to interact with and release and deal with emotional pressure, while during the day time I was instructed to scrub floors, make beds, tidy the play room and so on.

Please God, keep me and boys sane, I asked day and night. As every night, I continued to talk for an hour at least, in secret to my precious Maker, as Jesus was opening the door for my life to soar into His abundant life of love. However, I had to endure this tragic time and jump, with Gods help, over the hurdles while holding my two precious sons very closely to my bosom.

As I remembered God's promise, "Believe in me, for I am the Way, the Truth and Life." John 14:6, it was as though Jesus, through actions, was saying, "I want to give you a future" and I needed that desperately!

Yes two weeks slowly passed. My lawyer got temporary

possession of our house for me and my boys. Just days before we left the shelter, Christmas Eve and Christmas day, were a blur. However we enjoyed a beautiful Christmas Day meal, right in the middle of our negative crisis, thanks to the wonderful men and women that gave their time, support, love and effort. May God continue to bless them with His grace and mercy as much as they have blessed me and my children. For, God is Love and that is exactly what these men and women were and also gave. God was in our very midst through skillful untiring hands.

Chapter 30

December 28, 1988- It was time to return home again. On arrival home, a friend's husband changed the front door's lock, for privacy purposes. The boys and I had our home with our beds, our clothes and each other's company back again. Their father was forced to get lodging in an apartment, not me! All his venomous threats towards me had turned around to bite him in the butt. The memory of his words rang in my ears, "You're NOT getting the house! You're NOT getting my money! You're NOT getting the car! You're NOT getting the boys! You're a crazy woman!" He hated everything I was and stood for and he made no attempt to hide it.

Being 20 pounds lighter than two weeks earlier, my whole life, inside and out, looked brighter, and better. Another "dancing chicken" passing through my life was warmly welcomed. I had my faith in the invisible, Lord, Jesus, and He gave me a roof over our heads.

Financially, I was responsible for our utilities, food, clothes and gas. With working fulltime again, at my regular department store position and Mackenzie and Kirby attending school, things relaxed in our lives and we hardly noticed that Murrey wasn't around.

Previous to the separation, I had been saving money for a family vacation. For about two and one-half years of savings I collected close to $4,000.00 and that is what we lived off of for the next seven months.

Every other weekend, my children went to be with their father. During the week and every other weekend, my boys would be with me. Still every night, faithfully, I talked and talked to God, silently and privately.

I remember the weekends that my son's were away at their dad's. I was never able to stay in my home over night by myself. From childhood, I still had a terrible night-time fear. Every other weekend I would faithfully head for my widowed mother's apartment. She lived in a high-rise downtown. Because of being stricken by MS nineteen year's earlier, Mom was wheelchair bound since dad's passing a year earlier.

Even from her wheelchair, she was my fortress, strength and my saving grace, time after time. Most of the time on Friday evenings, I would take mom for groceries, bring her back home, take her up to her apartment and unload the bags of food. I would park my car and proceed indoors for the nights stay.

I learned also during these weekends of despair, without my children, that God's word, again, is truth. He says "He will only give us what we can handle." And "He always gives us a way out."

After sitting down in my mother's living-room chair,

the TV turned on, I would completely, mind, body and spirit, shut down. Not knowing how much time elapsed, I was like in an upright coma. I knew my mom was in the kitchen area, watching and putting food away. She never spoke to me. She just was present. Maybe she knew in her spirit that I was unable to converse at that time. I never heard or saw the television. I just sat there physically and mentally completely numb. God temporarily shut my body functions down! Through this I learned that depression overload is not only emotional, it can also be as physical as not walking, talking or thinking.

After about an hour of "shut down", I came back to full functioning ability and the evening was over. The television was then turned off, the couch made into a bed for me and our good nights were said. Bless my mother's sweet heart!

Chapter 31

My days at work continued. However, I was not completely out of the woods concerning safety. Shortly after we came home from the shelter, I was almost the victim, of a vehicle crash. As I travelled the hills and highways, in our fair city, by the grace of God, I noticed an odd rattle of grinding somewhere under my car. I didn't have a regular garage station for the repairs of my car but I felt I must look into this curious noise. As the noise got worse, I headed for the nearest, most familiar garage station I knew of. There, after a walk around inspection of my car by the mechanic, it was revealed that all the lug-nuts were loose except one lug-nut that was holding the front wheel on. Thank God I didn't crash from the wheel coming off coming down an incline or hurt my precious cargo, Mackenzie and Kirby!

I couldn't prove my husband's vandalism but I knew hatred when I saw and heard it.

Soon we were going through January and February of 1989. This is when God's precious Holy Spirit began gently prompting me further. Softly yet persistently, God was talking to me. With His silent voice speaking into my heart, over and over again, He told me to quit my job. At first I thought, that's crazy! There is no way possible I could do that. Who would support my children and me? However I knew with out a doubt that Mackenzie and Kirby were my very first priority and I needed them to know beyond a doubt, that I was not going to desert them in any way, shape or form. They were silently suffering and I somehow wanted to protect them from unnecessary feelings of abandonment.

If I was about to trust God, I had to trust Him all the way. Jesus had gotten me this far. He saved my mind, body and soul. He rescued me from a loveless controlling marriage. He gave me custody of my children. He saved me and my children from a car crash. He provided a roof over our heads. He provided the professional heads and hands along this treacherous path! Jesus had become my best friend and now He wanted me to trust Him again.

For two full months I disregarded and almost fought what God was saying to me. But slowly, time after time of hearing God's instructions, I found the faith that Jesus had planted deep within my soul, to respond positively to His instructions. I quit my position at the local department store.

I knew God wanted this for me and I knew also I had $4,000.00 in a bank account. I immediately, on quitting, visited the employment agency where I immediately learned that I qualified as a mature student and as such could enroll in a two year college course through the employment agency. This course would be paid for, plus a $400.00 a month living wage. Since I had the $4000.00 in the bank, I decided right there on the spot, that I would register immediately for September of 1989 classes.

I planned on using the money I had saved to live off of for the next six months and start receiving the $400.00 a month starting the coming September 1, 1989.

Also, God had been prompting me to quit for the last two months and now as I sat in the employment agency office, I understood why the Holy Spirit was so persistent. There on my application day I was informed by the employment agent that officially there was one more seat open and again, by the Grace of God, that was claimed by me. I love God's "dancing chicken's" so much.

My desire to be with my boys, as much as possible, was coming to reality. Two weeks after giving notice at work, I started going to school with my boys. I volunteered myself in both of their classes as a mom's teachers assistant and was always available to them. I secretly hoped the school would hire me on part-time, but that never came to be. For the next four months I wanted my children to know beyond a doubt that I was not going to leave them. I wanted them to know that I was there to protect and care for them. At night I kept praying, only now thanking the Lord for the evidence of His Hand on my children and my life.

For the time being, the house was ours and I had my children. My estranged husband's words were only threats, nothing more while God was putting a safety net under the three of us. Thank you, precious Savior for You are alive!

Chapter 32

Winter was going, spring was almost here. It was the middle of April and another desire was becoming very strong in me. For the last thirteen years of my marriage, my husband always fear mongered me by telling me that I was would probably have an accident or someone would crash into me while driving on the highway. Day or night, I was not safe. He repeatedly said that I would have either a flat tire, blow the motor or have a collision. This all meant that I was never allowed the freedom of highway driving without serious fear! Therefore I just didn't drive anywhere out of the city. After thirteen years of frightening, controlling statements, much hatred for his mercy-less condemnation resided deep within the walls of my mind and heart.

After thirteen years of me slowly dying inside from his negativity, I finally, with my growing faith in Jesus' leading strong hand, decided to fight for freedom and hope! My desire to drive on the highway was bigger than me. It had been four months since I had left him and now I knew I absolutely had to drive west to the neighboring city, via the highway, for my own sake.

April had come and I was up for the challenge. At first I asked two of the three women friends I knew to come with me for the weekend. They replied that they couldn't this month but would love to go in May. I felt very strongly that God was calling me to venture on the highway now in April, not May. I had to face my fears of highway driving. I had to! My two friends were worried for me but they knew I was serious. So my plans were made.

The weekend came. My children were at their dad's while I set out early Saturday morning. I had phoned ahead and reserved a room at a new, very nice hotel with a swimming pool and restaurant. I knew it was more than I should spend, but I felt strongly that is where God was leading me. He wanted me to trust Him.

As I set out on my hour and one half journey, the weather was calm and cool. The roads were clear and dry and it certainly was a beautiful April day. Thank you, Jesus for preparing the way.

I had driven approximately half way when suddenly I noticed some smoke coming out from under the hood of my car. What! What now! I carefully pulled over to the road side and turned the engine off. The very first thing that popped into my head was "My husband planned this." "He does NOT want me on the highway driving!" I didn't cry and I didn't panic. I just sat there for a couple of minutes after I opened the hood. There was smoke, no fire, thank goodness. With my engine off, hood open, I literally sat in my car and asked Jesus to help me know what to do.

Within, what seemed, to be only a few minutes or so, an old pickup truck with a man, woman and child, pulled up beside my car. The man yelled out the passenger side, asking me if everything was OK. I yelled back telling him briefly that smoke under the hood of my car had made me pull over.

Promptly, he got out and we both looked for the cause. I certainly didn't know the cause and he didn't seem to either. That is when he suggested that I start up the car, turn it around and follow him and his family back to the last garage on the highway. I did as he suggested, slowly and extremely cautiously. Luckily we only had to back track a couple of miles.

We came to a very rundown, almost vacant two door service station. There was no gasoline, no restaurant only a decrepit garage building. There I was instructed to pull up to the one overhead door, open the hood of my car, got out of the car and gazed awkwardly, not knowing what to expect. I certainly didn't know where this was going at all.

A country type older gentleman proceeded to take a look under the open hood. After only a few minutes, maybe five, the garage man told me that the smoke was harmless and had come from a, get this, a mouse nest in the lining of the car hood! I could hardly believe his words. So far in my inexperienced life, I had never heard of such a thing.

Then things got even crazier! I asked the mechanic how much I owed him for his service and time. Without a flinch, he responded "Two dollars should do it." He closed the hood and I gave him two dollars worth of quarters. Without even a goodbye, the family with the truck left and I was left standing there wondering what my next step was going to be.

What did just happen!? Was I possibly just entertained by angels? Had God Himself just intervened? Again it was if Jesus was saying loud and clearly, "Trust Me, Elizabeth and you will be safe."

With that unusual encounter, I had a decision to make. As I sat in my car I thought, "Do my husband's threats win and I go back home or do I continue to challenge my independence and keep on going west?" Within seconds I knew I chose a trip to hope, success and life. So instead of heading back home, I made a left hand turn, onward, to my weekend destination. Thank you, Jesus for being so near.

By the grace of God, the rest of my highway drive was smooth and uneventful. The sun shone brightly. The roads were dry. There was no wind and my car ran like a charm.

About an hour later I arrived at my city destination. Times before, I had been to this city, but not as the driver. First things first, as I followed the road signs and instructions I received earlier over the phone. I understood the road signs and found the hotel, which was big, new and beautiful. I parked the car and proceeded to check in. There I was in for yet another surprise. For some unknown reason to me, the cost of a nights stay was more than I expected and I had another, on the spot, decision to make. Do I pay the extra cost and stay the night or do I turn and run. Slowly but surely the decision was made. I stay! I was not going to sway now! By hook or by crook, I wanted to pass this weekend test and I knew I had Jesus as a Co-Pilot. He had brought me this far, so I just kept on trusting and believing. Suitcase in hand, I paid and made my way to my night's room.

In my room, alone, timid and a bit unsure, I lay on the bed and thanked my Savior for an eventful but very successful day. After deciding to actually go for a swim, I mustered up enough courage, left the room and went to the pool. I could hardly believe where and what I was doing, and it felt great!

I didn't swim very long, but enjoyed every moment of it. After only about half and hour or so I went back to my room to watch some television and make ready for bed.

As I entered the hotel room my room's telephone was ringing. Surprised by the call, I picked it up to find that I was the recipient of a long distant call from one of my two friends that I had asked to come along. This precious friend was the only person I talked to all evening, and she just wanted to know and hear that I was OK.

After a short conversation, I said "good night" and continued to turn the bed covers down. After the days events I was very exhausted, so I said my prayers, turned the lights out and slept soundly until morning.

Rising early Sunday morning, I dressed, packed again and went downstairs for breakfast. As I was enjoying breakfast, at a window table, I heard my name over the intercom. Believe me, when I heard my name being paged, I was one surprised guest. I went to the lobby desk where they instructed me to go and there, by the Grace of God, was another long distance phone call for me.

Another phone call! How precious my friends were and still are. I basically had only two girl friends and it turned out the call was my other girl friend. She too was checking on me, bless her caring heart! I couldn't believe it. Never before, have I felt that somebody cared. Now in twelve hours I was shown love by two people who did.

Now as I see it the "dancing chickens" were accumulating and I loved it.

Now I realized that if I had opted out for a cheaper hotel, my friends would not have known how to get in touch with me. Cell phones were not yet in the picture for people and my friends would probably have been very worried for me if they couldn't locate me.

Again, thank you Jesus, for giving me the strength to trust your will for me.

After a short conversation with my friend, I went back to my table and finished my breakfast. Through the window I noticed that it had snowed lightly overnight but for some reason this didn't bother me. With success behind me I became stronger and more determined of a complete successful road trip.

Leaving the parking lot my heart sang, my confidence soared and I believe, without a doubt, this truly was the beginning of a new road and destination in my life. My new life, hand in hand with God and a new sense of success in myself was proving to be very satisfying and I felt very happy about it!

Chapter 33

On arriving home again, the rest of April went smooth. My boys knew I was attending their school daily, taking turns within each of their classes. Every other weekend I would go to my mother's apartment while my children would go to their dad's home.

For the last three and half years, I faithfully talked to Jesus, in my thoughts as the last conversation before falling to sleep at night. Most times my thinking or silent conversation with God, turned out to be a least 45 minutes to an hour long. I always thought that after almost twenty years of praying my-self to sleep, God must have a sense of humor because as I was engaged in conversation for a long time, eventually the line would go suddenly quiet, as I would fall fast asleep on my end.

During all those years of praying my-self to sleep, my precious Maker took me, in my sleep to many places that I believe were part of heaven and showed me many wonders involving how Heaven works and is. In the late night hours, completely asleep, I would find myself, my spirit, in many places that seemed to be part of a city. There were streets with well kept, beautiful houses. There were important people making decisions in higher-up offices. There was an incredible body-part warehouse where I was shown different types of legs, arms, eyes, ears, mouths and bodies. The most significant body parts I remember were the different types of legs, which were very amazing.

On another occasion within a deep sleep, was when, I believe, I had the most incredible journey to see God the Father. When I saw God the Father, we didn't speak. I just stared in complete awe and I knew I was in the most High Place possible. I won't and can't describe what I saw, but the next morning when I awoke and looked at any person alive, I saw the face of God the Father in every face. Young, old or middle aged, I saw God's Holy image in every human face feature. Quite amazingly, God's Holy Bible, says that God made man in His Image, and guess what? By God's Grace, I believe I've seen what He means.

Surprisingly enough, on another nighttime adventure, I was the recipient of my own guardian angle. Again in awe, I stared open eyed, at the most beautiful, blond-brown, shoulder length, corn silk haired creature I have ever seen. I was totally taken back in speechlessness by her extensive, huge wing span. She was pure white, very large and extremely beautiful, like I said before.

Her mouth didn't move but I heard her tell me through thought waves that, she had been with me from the beginning. I remember staring so much at her enormous wings that I only partly focused on the rest of her. Never before had I witnessed such radiant beings, as those in the city of Heaven.

It seems as though, many nights that I was asleep after praying, was when the Holy Trinity would take my spirit away to another dimension to reveal Heaven's essence slowly but none the less, I believe, true reality.

Chapter 34

On the night my father, Lenard, died, I again was the recipient of yet another glimpse into heaven's realm. My father's passing was in the middle of November 1987. Now my father was raised in a Christian home, but unfortunately, it was a blended home with a step-mother and step sisters that somehow never really felt whole to my father. Lenard, my dad, had emotionally never gotten over his mother's death when he was nine years old and the new marriage situation. So again, unfortunately, as his life unfolded, it turned out that he was against the Good News of Jesus Christ.

My father's trust in his dad and God had been shattered at an early childhood age and it took until his dying day's to find the courage to change his mind and voice it with his mouth. Like I mentioned before, from sixteen years old to two years before dying, my father lived his life at the bottom of beer and whiskey bottles.

By the Grace of God, the last two years of dad's life were dry without alcohol and me as a brand new, born again Christian was on fire for God. I had a wide open playing field, alcohol free dad, to preach and persuade and hopefully turn to Jesus. I needed to know that we would see each other again, after we die, in heaven!

During these two very special years I got to know and love, for the first time, my sober, kind father. He was continually patient and sat quietly while I tried to tune him into his eternity path. However, on one dear occasion, he did tell me that the missionaries needed me in Africa and somehow I loved him for that. My sincerely wonderful father did love me and was getting the message of my gentle persistence. In those two years of visiting and emotional stabilization, dad and I formed a truly caring bond of love and appreciation for each other.

Thank you, Jesus, for the opportunity to get to know my father and dear loving friend, Lenard.

Within three months of turning 60 years old, my dad received by telephone the news that he had cancer. It was cancer of the esophagus and he died almost exactly three months later on November 17, 1987. His illness time was short and aggressive, but by the Grace of God, dad too asked Jesus into his heart.

On the event of Lenard's death, God showed me that He was there to hold my dying fathers hand while guiding dad home to his refuge. Once again, miracle after miracle occurred in my dad's life and un-expectantly in my life as well. In the early morning hours of November 17, 1987, my dad was taking his eternal walk through deaths door while I was fast asleep in my bed beside Murrey.

While I was in a very deep sleep and in my dreams, I

was walking in another realm beside another person. I could not see the other persons face or body but I felt the other person's presence. The atmosphere was darkness, as if nighttime. As we walked I looked ahead of me. In the dream and I saw that we were walking up a gradual incline amazingly towards a radiant illuminating brightness.

In the deepest of deep sleep, I was completely consumed in this occurring dream. I was also vaguely sensing something jarring my physical body. Rapid jabs against my back, slowly and grudgingly were bringing me out of the walking dream that I was experiencing, bringing me to murky consciousness.

On awakening, I could hear something ringing. As I resumed more consciousness, I knew it was the telephone. Murrey had been jabbing me in the back, trying to wake me up and was yelling at me to get up and answer the telephone. It was approximately 2:00 a.m. and the phone was in the kitchen.

Thank God for Murrey's laziness and persistence. I had been in such a deep sleep state that I may have continued on in my dreams walk, up into that amazing soft yet bright, loving light.

As I pulled myself out of bed, away from the dream and ranting husband, I answered the phone. Within seconds I heard from my dad's sister, my aunt, that my dad had just been pronounced dead.

I knew immediately that what I had just been experiencing in my dream was actually my dad's spirit that I was walking with. I knew without a doubt that Lenard, my troubled father, had before he died, asked Jesus into his heart and was now going home.

Dad, after death, had come to me, in my deep sleep, to see me and say farewell until we meet again. He was now on his way to his refuge, his Heavenly home. His earthly mission was done and now it was time for peace. Praise God for loving my dad like only God can. Love you, Jesus and thank you for saving my father, Lenard, even if it was on my dad's deathbed.

Believing that I knew without a doubt that my dad made it to the destination that I hoped for me and all my family, was indeed one more exceptionally beautiful miracle or "dancing chicken", that to this day brings tear drops of pure joy.

The next day at my mom's and dad's home, the family was gathering and it was there that I learned from my dad's sisters that just before dad went into a comma, my aunts had a conversation of Salvation with him. On his last leg in this world, without hesitation, dad asked Christ for forgiveness and to come into his heart, washing dad clean from all his burdens and sins. Then upon looking up at the hospital clock, announced that "There are eleven before me and I am number 12 and I'm ready to go" Next he then amazingly questioned his sister standing at the end of the bed about an angel, sitting in the chair beside his bed.

The chair, I was told actually had his oldest sister sitting there. Again without any hesitation he asked to be seated in the chair with the angel. As his first request was denied he requested it again, only this time more assertively almost demanding it. The nurse was called in and with a very excitable patient the bed to chair transfer was made. Within seconds passing in the angel chair, my father then collapsed into a comma. He was then laid into his bed and shortly after passed from this world into the next without fear or anxiety of any sort. Praise you, Jesus for my dreams conformation.

That was 1987, just two years after I became a born-again Christian and now the essence of many God inspired "dancing chicken's", or miracles seemed to be weaving through my life. "Flying monkey's" were becoming less interfering and active as Jesus was putting, piece by piece, of my life's puzzle in their proper places. With every fiber of my being, as my life was being transformed from desperate to inspired, I was in amazed awe and total appreciation of every glimpse into possible life happiness, for me.

God loves me and God loves you. We only have to ask Him into our lives and then trust Him. He will do the rest.

Chapter 35

Back to, as mentioned earlier, the adventurous trip in the first part of April 1989 to our fair neighboring city by my-self via the high-way was truly a beautiful success. I soon found my-self back in my daily and weekend routine, thereafter, with a new found faith in God and yes, myself.

Later in April of 1989, one evening on a regular, taking mom grocery shopping night, I had mom in her apartment, the food taken inside and was parking my car for the night. When I got back in my car to park it, I found myself talking to God's Son, Jesus as though He was sitting right next to me in the passenger's seat. For at least fifteen minutes, I sat there pouring out my hearts desires to the God that had rescued me over and over again. My previous numbness depression experienced in the past four months in my moms house armchair, had slowly dissolved and now I knew what my priorities were.

There I asked Jesus "What do I have to do to meet a loving, kind, Christian man that would be my best friend?"

I knew I didn't want to spend the rest of my life alone. My children were my greatest gift from Heaven, so far, but I wanted and needed a best friend to share my life also. Did I have to go to a bar to find a loving man? Did I have to go somewhere else for the right man?

I wanted a man, best friend first, that would love me for me, not for my car, not for my job, but for the only thing I had to give, and that was the love in my heart!

After crying, literally out loud to God's Holy Son, Jesus, I knew I didn't want any part of a meat market bar scene. I knew I didn't know any such single, best friend, Christian man but I did believe, "With God ALL things are possible." I looked in my rear view mirror, looking disapprovingly at the drinking establishment behind my car and knew, in my mind and in my heart, that I would never take a step towards or into such a building for any man. Drying my tears with my conversation over, I parked the car and went inside to spend the night with my sweet mother.

The spring disappeared, the months went by. Soon school was done for the year and still I was alone. God bless my mother for all the weekend overnight visits.

Now I have learned that prayer is one end of conversation and God somehow answering back is the other end. After my talk to Jesus in the car I had another dream that seemed very important also. I was shown my dad sitting behind a writing desk, writing something. Dad and his desk were somehow behind a clear veil or plastic glass. My dad was in a different place than me, not hurting but it looked like he was writing something concerning me, possibly doing an assignment concerning my and maybe his future. Mine on earth and his in heaven.

At the time of that dream I was very alone, except for my boys and gentle mother. Somehow I felt Jesus was in charge and God wanted me to know something about my dad.

Well dad was, I believe, writing possibilities into my future. Maybe dad had been given a mission in heaven and I was it. I do believe Christians have lives to live and duties to accomplish, given to them in Heaven, after death. God's word says many times that Heaven is a city. Praise God, for life is promised in the city of Heaven, after death!

Chapter 36

Beginning of August 1989 our home was sold and our housing arrangements came apart at the seams. With our home sold, my two children and I had to evacuate. With no where to go and four hundred dollars in the bank, I desperately needed a housing miracle and fast. Mackenzie, Kirby and I were just existing and living on a very short shoe string budget while eating macaroni and cheese with wieners. Please Lord, help us! Where were we going to live now?

With determination and a huge housing need pushing me, I decided I had better head down to our fair cities Welfare office. There it was made clear to me that since I owned a car even if it was twelve years old, I did not qualify for financial help. If I sold my $300.00 car, than and only then, they would be able to give me some money.

Whew, that didn't make much sense to me since I needed transportation for emergencies and to get me to college and back. That just didn't seem like an option to me, so in disbelief, I left the building and looked for another avenue of help.

The next office I ended up at was the office of the Low Rental Housing Association. It was now the second week of August 1989 and I knew without a doubt that financially my original $4000.00 was mostly gone and we were in a very serious, lack of money, situation.

With a serious face and overwhelmed heart, I walked into the Low Rentals Office where I was greeted by two women. One was young and the other, who now I know as Dez, was a middle aged woman. Embarrassed and with a statue hard face I proceeded to share my story of two little boys, no housing and only $400.00 in the bank.

As my horrifying scenario of our desperateness passed through my lips onto their ears, I crumpled like a rag doll emotionally into humiliating tears of anguish. I really was a wreck and I didn't know how I was going to keep my children fed and housed. Would I lose my children to poverty? Would I lose them to their father? No, please No God! Jesus, please send someone to help me!

Almost immediately, Dez went into action. She had felt the state of emergency I was in. She took me by the arm and proceeded to reassure me of housing as soon as possible. My name was to be put on the emergency list at the very top. Again there was another rescue for us being put in place. Again, God was using professionals to aide me and my children. Thank you, Dez! Thank you, Jesus!

With red eyes and a renewed sense of hope, my hearts load was lightened. I recomposed myself, turned to go and said "thank you".

That's all I could do. Again I had been helpless and now somehow, hope was back in the picture. I didn't know how long before a home would come available but I knew God had the ball rolling. To me this was truly another huge "dancing chicken" and so I believed and I trusted, again.

Since the day our home had been sold I had been searching the newspaper daily for an apartment, something cheap with at least two bedrooms and with-in our local area. With-in days after my meeting with Dez, I read of a basement apartment close to the boy's school and it was only $300.00 a month. At that rate I would be able to afford one months stay. After checking it out I decided that it filled our need. It was in the basement and very small but it was one block from Mackenzie's and Kirby's school.

I called the number on the advertisement and later met with the caretaker. On seeing the suiet, I paid the lady caretaker and the apartment was reserved for us starting September 1.

A lot seemed to be going on. The boys and I were planning to start school and I college after the long weekend. I started receiving my college wage of $400.00 a month, September 1 and we also had to execute the furniture move. Another whirlwind, whew!

Thank goodness for my only brother, Jonathan. He had a truck and offered to help me with the move. Thank you, Jonathan. August passed and September 1 was here. The dwelling move was underway. By the end of the day, our tiny, somewhat cold, basement apartment was overflowing of multiple furniture staples, garbage cans, rakes, a lawnmore, beds, a couch, kitchen supplies and a table with chairs. We were undated and over run with mass clutter with only a narrow path to the bedrooms. As I looked at the environment of our new temporary home, I felt I was seeing again the sour flavor of poverty once more in my life.

However, in the privacy of those four walls, I closed my eyes with tears rolling down my cheeks and thanked the very Jesus that had saved me from death only three years earlier. So far my children were in my custody, clothed, fed and still had a roof over their sweet young heads. Plus I was still alive to love them with all my heart and to hold them tenderly through this painful ordeal.

Thank you, Master Physician, Counselor and Provider. Thank you for adopting me and my children into Your Fold.

Chapter 37

The move accomplished, the boys back in school, me on course at the college and the divorce slowly coming to the pinnacle final settlement, it seemed life was beginning to get some kind of order and I was grateful.

The divorce had taken from December to October with my main conviction to just escape from the loveless, Godlessness negativity and control.

On one occasion early in January with-in my lawyer's office meeting, I was sitting facing my lawyer, as she was displaying great ammunition against Lenard and his case. She told me I could get the boy's, the house for my own, the car, the furniture, bank accounts, RRSP's, child support and alimony if I would only let her fight for me. She had fire in her words and meant business. She was emotionally strong and aggressive and I know beyond a doubt, she could have won hands down.

However, as she was finished her injection of fire of advice, there was silence and I felt in my spirit that we weren't alone. It was as if Jesus Himself was sitting behind me, softly coaching my every decision.

At the end of her fighting words, with a very strong possibility of winning everything financial, I heard a still, silent, yet strong voice penetrate the ears of my heart. God was telling me "Don't fight" and at that moment I repeated what I knew God was speaking and directing me to do.

My lawyer was briefly speechless and I knew I had offended her. I pray, "Please forgive me, Mam, but I have learned to fear and trust the unseen living God, for He knows best".

My lawyer kept me on, but she wasn't happy with me. I didn't fight for the mortgage free house. I didn't fight for alimony. I didn't fight for RRSP's.

Basically, I just didn't fight. I just wanted my two beautiful boys and my freedom back to live and grow. That's all and that is exactly what I got. Starting October 1, 1989, through the divorce agreement, I was the recipient of, praise God, most importantly custody of my children, some furniture of our previous home, almost one third of the homes value, $18,000.00, a twelve year old car and $150.00 per child, per month of child's maintenance allowance from Lenard.

That meant that I, for the next two years, was to have a total of $700.00 a month income. With the house money, I decided to purchase a smaller, newer car that hopefully would be more reliable for my boys and me. With out a job or so called "career" to support us, we were still very much in God's hands. We just had to trust and watch things unfold.

Chapter 38

September 1989

One of my friends that had telephoned me on my high-way travels in April called me to tell and invite me for a supper and meet with one of her man friends, who was single. It was nine months since I left Lenard and Gloria my friend, bless her heart, thought I was ready to start meeting men. She said this man was nice. At first I was hesitant because I had ten foot emotional walls all around me. But then I remembered my conversation with Jesus only 4 months previous, so later I agreed to meet him over supper.

The date was set. September 22/89 I went to my girl friends house and there met Edwin. Now because of my first husband's faith rejection towards me, I definitely had major spiritual concerns of whom I would even consider a possibility for partnership. Not just any man was partnering with me again. He had to have Jesus and the Holy Trinity in his heart and it had to be obvious.

First we were introduced. Ok, fine. Then we conversed awhile. Then it was time to eat. We sat down and quite new to me, for the first time ever, Gloria asked me to say Grace. First surprised by this, I proceeded to do as asked and then however, the evening took on a different course of action. Again Praise God, The Holy Spirit was there with us. Seemingly offended by the "religious" act of praying before the meal, the supper time air went cold. Edwin could hardly wait to leave my company.

No matter how nice he may have been there absolutely was no so called "religion" in that mans agenda. With all said and done, Edwin left my friend and me about 8:00 o'clock. With plan one ditched, my very charming host and friend put plan two into action. Little did I know that in the next hour, by the grace of God, I was to meet my next new wonderful, soul mate husband!

With Edwin out the door, Gloria was on the phone, this time to call a man named Randall. By this time it was coming close to 9:00 o'clock and he certainly wasn't expecting such phone calls but to my now delight, he was home resting.

Gloria had told me how much Randall and I were, alike. We shared similar qualities like going to church regularly on Sundays as well as that he had two children that he was responsible for also. That sounded like he possibly had potential. "However", Gloria hesitatingly told me, "He is Catholic." I guess because I was protestant, Gloria thought "Catholic" may be a problem.

Now Randall and I, as husband and wife, chuckle at Gloria's sincere concern of blended "faith" lines. That was so sweet of her and at one time in history that may have been a problem, but Randall's "Jesus" was and is my "Jesus" and together we rest in His Hands.

When Gloria called him at 8:45 he was resting and had to be gently asked or coaxed to come over. Maybe he could come for pie and coffee? We still hadn't had dessert and we could share with him. At first he thought no, but shortly with encouragement, rethought it. Possibly because of my friend's persuasiveness and enthusiasm, the evening was still not over. Bless her match making heart!

The phone was hung up and we waited. Little did we know it but, Randall we found out later, circled the block three times having a tug a war, should he or shouldn't he, come over? Finally 9:15 came and Randall was at the door and yes, my now soul mate, best friend, arrived.

As he entered the living-room I noticed his stature. He was tall, strongly built, very handsome and had a very sweet smile. His eyes were gentle blue and his handshake firm. Still, I had no intention to let my walls down without him earning it. Gloria sat between us and viewed that evening a very sincere, honest, careful conversation between us. Our conversation seemed to flow almost effortlessly.

All too soon the pie and coffee was eaten and emptied and it was getting late. We said our cordial goodbyes and I knew deep within my heart that this new Christian man friend was certainly a strong possibility for my future. The two last hours had flown by.

Thank you, Jesus. Could it be possible that God crossed my life's paths with Randall's for a very special reason? Maybe this was another "dancing chicken"? I just kept on praying and trusting.

Chapter 39

It was now the end of September and one week had almost gone by since meeting Randall. I had not heard from him. Was he interested? Did he care?

As hectic as the last month was, getting my children back in school and starting to attend college myself, our move the beginning of September, I then received a phone call from the Low Rental Association on September 15th and as of October 1st, we were provided with half a duplex. That meant another move, however this time, just across the street. Thank you, Jesus. You are Forever Faithfull!

September 28th I picked up the duplex keys and low and behold I received a telephone call the same day at supper time. This time it was Randall calling and we ended up talking for close to an hour. I knew I needed help for the move but there was no way I would ask a man I hardly, if barely new. Things were moving and moving fast. I had another move to undertake with basically no one to help.

On September 28th when I picked up my house keys, I decided to use $100.00 from my $400.00 September college check to hire a moving van with two men to move the furniture and boxes. My cousin's wedding was planned for the day before my moving date and I planned to attend that also. By the Grace of God and unbeknownst to me, before the move, at my cousin's reception, I met up with a close childhood friend, that offered to help me move into my duplex the next day. I had told her briefly that I was planning a household move the next day and I was basically doing so by my-self. I had to wash down the cupboards, unpack numerous boxes, sort room by room furniture then move furniture and belongings to their proper places within the house.

I had prayed for God to some way help me and by sending Maureen, He did. I had no idea anyone the night before at a wedding would ever offer to help me.

Thank you again, Father and forever bless Maureen's loving heart! She had no ideal how much I needed her help. Thank you!

October 1st was here and my children and I were moved into a warm, plain, yet beautiful above ground duplex. My two boys shared a bedroom and I had my own. The rent charged me was one quarter my monthly income of August 1989, which came to $97.00 a month. That included utilities and a basement with another bathroom and bedroom plus an unfinished recreation-room for storage. My boys had a fenced back yard to occupy their time with hockey sticks and soccer balls.

Paying $97.00 a month rent meant that we would have $300.00 a month for food, gas, car insurance and miscellaneous. The Low Rental Association made it possible that my children and I could afford to exist.

Monthly income of $400.00 from my college wage wasn't much income a month but by the Grace of God, we had just enough. The total of $300.00 child support money that started to come in our household after

September 1989, was for Mackenzie's and Kirby's school fees, books, summer and winter clothing, medical, sports and any other costs pertaining to them. By the Grace of God my monthly rent due was one quarter of my college wage.

Wow, this duplex after the apartment, seemed to be deluxe accommodations and I appreciated every square inch of it! We were living in extreme poverty but our surroundings pleaded otherwise. Thank you, Jesus, for abundant miracles and "dancing chickens" that only God Himself can orchestrate. Truly I am eternally grateful!

My "flying monkeys" were becoming less and less and the hope and faith building in my mind and soul was overflowing with great joy! My cup was running over and I was free from control and negativity. Moment by moment I was overcoming anxiety and found myself daily yearning for the happy surprise events and miracles to unfold in my life like the opening of vibrant, soft petals of a gorgeous tropical flower. What I was learning was that relationships are what are important, firstly Jesus' friendship than all the other colorful people God brings into our lives. I had been taught that God the Father, Jesus, and the Holy Spirit is, Love beyond anything in our natural world.

If our biological father on earth loves us, it was being

proven to me slowly but surely, that God the Father in Heaven, loves us even more, even through life and beyond into eternity. Now eternity is a long, long time and I choose Heavens abundant eternity.

    Thank you Father, precious God for your loving Son, Jesus.

Chapter 40

After the boys and I got settled into our duplex, Randall and I became more acquainted by telephone. Many an evening, after our busy lives routine and, Mackenzie and Kirby were tucked into bed, Randall and I talked literally for hours.

During one of our now frequent phone calls, he asked me to accompany him to the movies. I was thrilled and responded positively. The whole evening of our date, I was treated kind and respectfully. We didn't hold hands and neither one of us assumed anything. Not once did he make a move at me. We just talked and laughed while enjoying each other's company.

Our first night out was coming to a close and the perfect gentleman Randall was and is, after walking me to the door, bent slightly over, said "good night. Thank you for a wonderful evening." and tenderly touched my chin and kissed me gently on my cheek.

I could barely believe that I was worthy of such a kind, gentle, gorgeous man. We were so alike in so many ways and it didn't end there, he seemed to be interested and agree with many of my opinions of life. To be treated with dignity, in a loving way, penetrated my very soul, and being.

Soon Randall was coming over Friday and Saturday evenings. There we would many times enjoy a meal, talk and have fun with the kids. When he wasn't at my house, we were on the phone and the more we talked, the closer I felt to him. I had never met a man so patient, sincere and loving.

I know beyond a doubt that God Himself sent this caring Christian man to be part of my boys and my life. How possibly could almost the very first man I was introduced to be such a perfect match, mind, heart and physically.

I joke with Randall to this very day that I was attracted to him because he had vivid blue eyes and he was taller than me. He knows I am quite tall but tells me in fun that I fell madly in love with him the first time I laid eyes on him. He didn't fall in love with me for about two month into our relationship and he sticks to that story.

Still after many, loving years of marriage, we fondly are reminiscence of our joyful and playful September beginning together.

Thank you, Jesus, for answering my open hearted sincere prayer, from only months earlier, in front of that bar.

The winter months passed by while my new man friend and I got more and more acquainted. Never before was I so amazed at another person's integrity and gentleness. The more time we spent together the more I fell in love with the man of my dreams. The emotional walls were literally melting from my sides. I fell in love with his simple, honest and caring charm. I was getting to know the internal part of him, the part we can't see, and I found myself also falling in love with him for his loving spiritual make-up.

The very core of his heart had Jesus at the centre and together we were one, like two matching pieces of a puzzle, fuelled by the same Holy Trinity. He treated me with respect while always listening to my views both secular and spiritual. He always treated me as though I was somehow special and to this day still carries my every heart desires and me highly on a pedestal. Basically he treats me like a princess worthy to be pursued and I love him even more as time passes, just for that.

About four months of learning about each other, it started. We became intimate. I knew he was more than a person just passing through our lives. His unique specialness to me eventually led from one thing to another, emotionally and yes, physically. Our love for each other was at times uncontrollable and our physical romance was tender while we were on fire for each other.

This physical romance went on for about a month only to come to an abrupt stop. As a Born Again Christian, I was in bed sleeping when I had a visitation from Jesus in my sleep. I could see Jesus coming down from the ceiling and His head was turning side to side motioning "no". Immediately I woke up and knew I had just been guided by God Himself, again. Jesus was saying "no" to my physical intimate moments with Randall and I knew also I HAD to obey.

My prayer life was still very prominent and vital in my

life for daily decisions. The past six years of my life had been governed by the Holy Spirit and God's way for me and I knew I had no choice but to share my latest vision of Christ to my loving Randall. I knew the physical romance had to abate. Giant questions loomed heavily over my head. What would Randall say? How would he react to me? Would he leave me? Would he think I was crazy? Would I loose him? Only God knew the answers to these dark questions but I knew I MUST stop our physical romance.

Dear Lord, please continue to be with us.

The "flying monkey's" were being overcome in my life and I didn't want to jeopardize any possibility of more "dancing chicken's" coming into my life by disobeying God now.

Shortly after the vision, I did it. I told Randall. With God's grace, my very loving man friend, informed me that he was willing to wait for my approval or better yet, Gods approval. As Christians we both knew that pre-martial sex was not a God advised plan for anyone and my wonderful Catholic man was also rooted deeply in his Christian Spirituality.

Over and over again, I deeply thank my precious Savior for putting the right man in my life. Previously living a life of negative spousal rejection, I wanted and needed a God loving and fearing man in my new life. Now the Catholic man sent to my very front door, both loved me with his heart, mind and soul, and feared and loved the Almighty Yeweh like I did. God certainly is Good and I praise Him.

Our romantic life was still very affectionate, loving, respectful and truly wonderful, however, there was no sex. By our sexual abstinence, Randall proved to me, again that his sincerity in our relationship was something I could trust and cherish. He was attracted to my childlike faith in Christ's truth, my humor, sincerity and integrity. Basically, he proved to me that he loved me for my heart and I in turn, loved and trusted his heart.

Thank you, Randall.

Soon the summer of 1990 arrived. School for my children and my-self had gone well. Life with my wonderful Christian man friend was growing leaps and bounds. The intensity of our relationship was leading us closer and closer together as we kept on talking.

Finally one summer evening a funny but wonderful event took place. The boys were spending the weekend over at their dad's home, while Randall and I were again, just sitting on the couch talking, when with out any formal notice, Randall commented quite surprisingly. "When, we get married…."

Not knowing if I heard him correctly, I looked at him and responded. "Did you just propose to me?" and with love and mischief in his clear blue eyes he responded, "Yes, I believe I did just that!" The radiation of pure excitement swept over my total being and without a moments hesitation or thought, I said with glee "yes" and he was the recipient of somewhat of a bear hug and a long enduring kiss.

Another "dancing chicken" and my life was about to take a beautiful bend in the road for cherished true love.

Thank you, again, precious Lord and Savior. You not only saved me from dyeing but now I was also to be the recipient of Heavenly sent happiness and Godly Love within a marriage with a Godly man.

Needless to say, that weekend was perfect in every way.

Chapter 41

August 1990 was here and Randall and I were verbally engaged. The next step was the ring on my finger, how exciting! The middle of the month came and Randall swept me off my feet and took me downtown to a fine jewelry store. There with Randall's and God's blessings, I picked out a modest but beautiful gold wedding set.

With a loving tender twinkle in his eyes, my new husband to be, drove us to a picturesque quiet park down by the trains, where down on one knee I was officially the recipient of a very romantic proposal.

With romance, wedding and sparkling love in the air, my emotions were erupting. First there were tears, then laughter, then more tears while soft tender kisses were exchanged and my hair was being stroked gently while being held tightly against Randal's chest. Love, real love, I don't believe happens all the time when two adults are joined as one, but with Jesus at the centre of our relationship, this truly was the start of a tender, long lasting, real love relationship called marriage.

That was a remarkably beautiful summer, now etched deeply within my heart. As a newly engaged woman, September was here again and my children and I were booked back into school for yet another year of learning.

It wasn't long at all after school started that Randall and I were starting to make plans for our big event. "When" should we tie the knot was definitely a big decision that we somehow had different ideas about. Randall thought possibly the following summer for a small wedding. I agreed about the small wedding part but somehow next summer was just too far away.

This time around, I was intrigued with a crystal clear winter's day wedding and I knew there would be time available during our school's winter break. Then also our four young children could be closely involved on our very special day.

After discussing the winter-time fairytale coming event with Randall, I was over-joyed when my groom agreed to the idea whom also was enthusiastic about it. Emotions high for both of us, January 2nd, 1991 was booked for the gala day.

After my divorce dust settled, I had $5,000 tucked away in the bank. Randall had been living in a tiny two bedroom bungalow in a near by hamlet which he sold to pay out his mortgage. He also had $5,000.00 left over to put aside. We then had a total of $10,000.00, to use as a down-payment, for a home of our own.

Praise God, another exciting new start! Truly that was another beautiful "dancing chicken". As happy as we were, the hard work had only begun.

There was tons of homework as five of our family was in school of some kind, two of our boys were in hockey, Randall and I had marriage classes at the church and we had to find a five bedroom house. That's not even mentioning the bag lunches and suppers that had to be prepared, let alone the aftermath of dishes and house chores.

Many times I prayed: "Holy Father God in Heaven, please provide mental calmness and also please give me the energy to survive". My so called plate in life was extremely full and with great awareness and prayer, I tried frantically to stop the overload from falling off.

With Randall's continual love and support, we were stronger in all ways. With three hectic months now passed and a house bought, the school's winter break was upon us and by midweek, right after Christmas, I would be taking on the name of Mrs. Randall Soffit. The excitement was certainly mounting while I was floating down a very strong, wide current river of blessed delightedness.

The big day, January 2nd, was here and we became our very own "Brady Bunch" or perhaps more like the military? With one bathroom and six people, the mornings, before work and school, were confusing to say the least. About ten minutes was allowed per person, per morning bathroom visit. Showers were short and furious or else done the night before. Even at ten minutes per person are day started at 6:00 a.m., promptly.

As I am sure with any "blended" family, the relationships with-in had to be built from the ground up. It was at times, seemingly impossible to achieve and difficult to adjust to new live-in step-siblings and step-dad and also step-mom parenting. New to each one of us our patience and tolerance was stretched and tried to the limit. But with love and persistence we did settle in. By the Grace of God we managed and most of our activities and responsibilities were met by all.

Chapter 42

With-in a few months after our wedding we were fairly settled in and again I experienced the hand of God reaching into my life. This time God had a message from my dad directed towards me and my Jesus trusting husband, Randall.

Our house had five bedrooms in it, one for each child and one in the basement for Randall and me. The month of March was ending and Randall and I were sound asleep while warmly tucked in bed. The morning hours were closing in and I was in for an amazing surprise.

Close to 4:00 a.m. I was suddenly awakened with a soft kiss on my cheek. Immediately on contact I sat upright fully aware while seeing my husband sound asleep beside me and also seeing that there was no visible person in the room with us. In my spirit, I knew without a doubt, that my deceased dad that came to me in my dreams twice earlier, had again somehow been here in our new home with my new husband beside me, to signal in the gesture of a kiss on my cheek, that Lenard my father approved of the man I married.

Somehow the dream of seeing my dad behind a clear veil, only two years earlier, writing something for me at a writing desk, had totally unfolded. Perhaps it was his job in the afterlife to map out happiness for his distraught little girl as his own acceptance and way into his own brilliant, God loving eternity.

I believe I know beyond a doubt, that Lenard, my dad had come to kiss me saying: "Congratulations Elizabeth. Carry on and be blessed in everything you do in life with this gentle husband that I sent you. Randall loves you and will take good care of you. I want you to know that God loves you and so do I".

Jesus is the way, the truth and the life and again I thank the very Holy Father God that made me, for Saving Lenard, my dad, from the Fires of Hell. His entire life on earth was an uproar and drunken disgrace but on dad's dying mattress in the hospital, dad asked Jesus into his heart and Lenard was born spiritually anew, shedding his chains of ugly bondage. Again I am learning that "Nothing is impossible with God" if we only believe.

As for our busy daily responsibilities wanting to fall off of our plates, by the Grace of God we managed most of our activities and the years gradually unfolded day by day, week by week and yes we even had a bit of time for housework.

Meanwhile as life unfolded for us as a married couple, our spiritual life kept growing also, first of all nightly with my head on my pillow talking to Jesus but also along side my spiritual soul mate husband and best friend, Randall Soffit.

I knew our genuine happiness was the absolute result of nightly Jesus conversations that I started in 1984, as a Born Again, Christian. It was through reading God's Holy Word, trusting it and my personal prayer life with the Holy Trinity that I was able to stay healthy, hopeful and blessed beyond measure. Overcoming obstacle after obstacle and having joy in all area's of our lives, I know is the outcome of intercessory prayer and growing faith.

Human words can not describe my indebted appreciation. Life unthinkably horrid, painful and leading to destruction was taken off my life's plate and pure sweetness and abundance of all goodness was put in its place. Thank you, Precious Jesus!

More changes were heading our way. Again by the hand of God, Randall was to receive a new job and site. Now Randall had his "Auto-body Mechanic" ticket as his education degree and had been working in very unhealthy chemical environments painting vehicles for most of his life's career. It was by word of mouth from another mechanic that he learned of a career opportunity at the military base near our home town. There were other men planning to apply and we at the time, of the posted advertisement, were on a short summer vacation.

Two days before the career posting advertisement was to be pulled out of circulation, we got back home to find on our answering machine a short but vital message for our future. That Monday coming in two days was the closing deadline for applications and Randall patiently had been waiting for literally months for the time to apply. Now was his opportunity and we almost missed it. It seemed that Jesus didn't want us to miss it either and here we were just in the nick of time.

Needless to say, very bright and early Monday morning, my sweet husband was at the Employment Office, filled out forms and then continued to his regular work day employment.

His present working conditions of auto-body work was full of paint fumes and hazardous chemical solutions. Most days he would come home from work with paint fumes on his breath and paint stains on his work clothes. We had no health benefits through his work and his pay was less than meager. By most peoples definitions we were a low-income family with six mouths to feed and a house yet to be paid for. However, Randall and I had an all powerful, all knowing Jesus that told us that with Him, all things are possible if we only believe and have faith. So with prayer and supplication, we kept on navigating out of need, redirecting our path into something more abundant.

The military "vehicle painter" would be definitely a move in the right direction. Randall applied the last day possible and then we waited, and waited, and waited.

Four weeks went by and yet no response was heard back. We know now that the military is not usually ever in any hurry for their decisions and this was no different.

Finally, two months passed by. It was October 1994 and Randall had almost given up on any employment change.

Then it came. The army was phoning Randall about the position he so dearly wanted. Praise The Lord! An appointment for an interview was made and things were beginning to happen, fast. Within a week's time, Randall learned that out of all the other applicant's, he was the only one with a Journeyman's Ticket and that ticket was his ticket "in".

Again, here was another "dancing chicken" showing up at our door-step. Thank you, God. We love it when our Maker sprinkles our lives with miracles. They are so delicious and exciting.

Another week went by after the interview with wonderful news the second week. Hooray! Randall got the job! His salary increased, we would have health benefits and mostly needed, the militaries safety paint overalls, paint masks and equipment were the best known available. My husband was to receive a healthy painting future for his career and we didn't take that lightly.

Jesus loves us and I know from experience, that He wants the very best for us physically, emotionally and spiritually.

Chapter 43

Five busy family, full years had passed by quickly while we lived in our first Soffit home. When Randall received his new job position we became interested in relocating to a more developed home. My brother, Jonathan, was trying to sell his home and this was interesting to us. In Jonathan's home was four bedrooms, a finished basement, large kitchen, large living-room, side driveway, automatic sprinklers, two bath-rooms, and for Randall, a beautiful, two car garage.

The house move looked favorable to us but I had no idea what else was going to change besides our house number.

April 1995 we purchased our second home. Within weeks, my oldest son, Mackenzie, came to me very timidly and asked me if he could move in with his dad. At first his words were like a knife in my heart. I couldn't believe my aching ears. I knew his dad could offer him the material stuff of life, like new clothes, more expensive food, his own room, a fancy two storey house and new cars, all which was mostly a much more affluent life style. I knew also with some parental guilt, that Randall and I couldn't anywhere near meet that standard. We drove old cars, shopped Value Village and sale racks and budgeted for food, possibly all because I was not a career woman.

Everything was expensive and Randall, bless his giving heart, worked hard at an honest day's job only to just make ends meet.

The things I wanted mostly in life, I had now and that was to be loved whole- heartedly by the man of my dreams, a true Christian man. To be cherished and cared about, to receive a husband and partner that at all times respected me, for me. Randall never put a price tag on my worth as a person.

As the years fell away, I just fell more and more in love with him because he nurtured my mind, heart and soul moment by precious moment with gentle, soothing encouragement and support.

I heard my son's piercing words and I knew that if I really loved him, I would have to let him go. He had lived with Randall and me for five full years and now maybe it was his dad's turn to enjoy his presence. Knowing that my son's expenses could be met better by a career father and career step-mother, all I could answer was "Yes, if you're sure."

Mackenzie, my son, I'm sure believed he would be happier where there was money, assets and no step-kid's. My faith life, in those years married to my son's dad, was like mixing oil with water. My ex-husband showed he was a non-believer while ridiculing my faith in Jesus, however, I knew from beyond a doubt, that Jesus is alive and living.

I knew Mackenzie would possibly be persuaded to fight Christianity or be scared of it, but I prayed "God forbid that from happening." I, through many life and death "flying monkey's" in my past life, knew prayer and the Holy Trinity had already won the war. Again, I put my faith into action and believed for a good outcome.

With tears in my eye's and sorrow mixed with faith in my heart, I gave Mackenzie a tight, long hug and told him I love him and always, no matter what, will.

Within a month's time from that conversation, my two young sons moved to their new home. It was if there had been a death in the family. A family home once bursting at the seams with energy was suddenly large and quiet. Randall's daughter, Laurie, decided to move to her mother's house and Ryan, Randall's son, was left alone with Randall and me. Ryan didn't say with his mouth but his body language and quietness told us that he felt very abandoned and slightly shunned while being left behind by all the other siblings.

Randall and I loved all our children and we had done the best we could for five years. Our family world, as we knew it was falling in all different directions. Now what? Please Jesus, help us and our children.

Chapter 44

Little did I know it at the time but I was about to start a career in an area that I had basically never before considered. When our children dispersed from our new home, in the summer of 1994, I was working at a Safeway's store in the area. I continued that until December 1995. The position I held was that of a courtesy clerk for almost three years but apparently Jesus had new plans for me.

First our house almost emptied out and then after a few months my husband had a serious talk with me about my schedule of work. He informed me very honestly that he had not married me for us to be passing each other at the doorway at 5:00 p.m. With him coming home from work at 5:00 p.m. and me going to work at 5:00 p.m., it just wasn't going to be ok. Evenings and the weekends were mostly when I had to work. He worked Monday to Friday during the days and he wanted me to somehow find a way to do the same.

After thinking it over, I took a leap of faith. I gave my

notice and December 31, 1995 was my last shift as a courtesy clerk.

Not knowing what I was qualified for, I thought perhaps a job as a foster parent would be a good possibility. I liked children and I knew people got paid to take care of distraught children situations. I needed a paying job plus I could be in a home environment. Our home was almost empty and me being a mother, a caregiver was probably my strongest talent.

Randall, in his first marriage, had been a foster parent and remembered clearly the stress and heavy responsibility it had been at times for him and his ex-wife. He informed me of some of the difficulties involved but agreed to look into it again if I felt I wanted to try this.

We signed up for foster parenting classes in January 1996. After three months of instruction and then testing, we passed, received a formal certificate and again our direction was to be altered.

It was the middle of April 1996 and I decided to go to a half-time bingo game at a local bingo establishment. Now about once every two months or so, I would do this and always found that there were few empty seats available half way through the evening, at intermission. Therefore I always ended up sitting where ever there was room.

On this particular April night, I found myself sitting next to a lady, that a year earlier, was one of my co-workers at Safeway's. We saw each other and then struck up a conversation.

First we got reacquainted, then, began talking about what each of us was presently doing in our lives. I found out she had opened a preschool in a school setting. I told her about my husband and I taking the foster parenting program and the rest is history.

As I was revealing, she was thinking. Before I knew it she continued to enlighten me with yet another career choice. She asked me if I had ever considered being a Nanny/House-Keeper? Actually that was the first time I had ever heard of a local job like that in our community and I was quite intrigued.

She continued to tell me of a family that had made personal calls to churches and pre-schools, asking for help to fill their Nanny/House-keeper position. The family searching had called her pre-school, had talked to her and now she was passing on the invitation of employment to me.

I asked her of the duties, the hours of working and the wages. I couldn't believe it! I would work Monday to Friday, 8:00 a.m. to 4:30 p.m. The monthly wage was a little more than that of Safeway's monthly wage and I would have the weekends off.

Now I thought that sounded pretty good. Praise God!

With the bingo games starting in the next couple of minutes, we exchanged telephone numbers, said goodbye, good luck, and went on with our evening.

Within two weeks of my "bingo" visit, I was seated in the living-room of my first "Nanny/house-keeper" client's home for an interview that was the start of my "Nanny/house-keeper" career. There I met two beautiful children, a boy and a girl, three and one years old. The parent's were a husband and wife teacher team who interviewed me for about an hour. They were polite, friendly and very aware of good parenting.

By the end of the month of April, I had been hired for $800.00 a month starting August 18, 1996.

Chapter 45

New Careers

Nanny/housekeeper and Writer

The middle of August 1996 was here and I went to my new house-hold Nanny position. There the parents and I interacted and talked frequently, getting to know each other. The last week of August, outside in their backyard, something quite incredible happened.

As the dad and I were talking, the sun was hot and brilliant. The backyard was deep, green grass and bushes. Colorful potted flowers were everywhere. The children were playing close by and I was standing in talking distance of my new employer. In the middle of conversation, a large beautifully colored butterfly came flying by. However it didn't fly pass us, it actually landed square flat on my right shoulder. It just sat there as time seemed to stop. Our conversation immediately stopped and we both took heed of its timely presence. For almost a full minute it just rested on my shoulder and entertained us, fluttering its beautiful wings.

As quietly as it landed, it again became air-born and gently fluttered over to my left shoulder. With complete grace, it again, just sat there, fluttering its gorgeous, large wings. As another quiet, timeless minute passed, the kids, their father and I, were clearly amazed at this unique happening.

As the butterfly flew from shoulder to shoulder, again, an amazing thing transpired, within my heart and mind. As the butterfly was passing directly in-front of me, my heart heard the word "Grandma". The word was very strong and I immediately knew God was telling me that my deceased Grandma, Louise, who died one year earlier who was also a very faithful Born Again Christian, was sending a blessing into my new career and position.

Praise, You, precious Jesus! I didn't know where this career choice was taking me but I knew Jesus and Grandma Louise consented and I was in God's plan for me.

A couple of weeks passed and school was in full swing. I was now a full-time Nanny/housekeeper. I suppose there are people that consider such a position very low on the professional totem pole of careers, but in my heart and mind, as a follower of Jesus, I felt, very honored to serve humanity in a child and home care-giving environment. I had no idea that what I had valued as the most important thing to me all my life, was now sprouting into a possible career. Thank you, God.

While I was visiting one day with the mom and dad, before they left for school, the dad informed me of one of his hobbies. I had never met anyone that wrote poetry and also children's story books, until now. I was intrigued, curious and impressed. I listened and filed the information somewhere deep within my inner being.

In the middle of September 1996, one morning, I was going about my work cleaning and tiding in the house, when my eyes fell on a piece of paper laying on the kitchen table, with a poem on it. Next to that was a folder with a children's story title on the cover. I just had to look inside, only to find the contents of a story book. I read both, the poem and the children's story. It was as if a seed was sown right at that moment, into my life. My boss had never been published, as far as I knew, but his effort was sincere and this made a huge impact on me.

As I sat there reading this art, I seriously wondered if I was capable of writing also.

Perhaps poems, perhaps stories were in me also. I felt strongly that I had to try.

I closed the folder, continued to tidy the table top and went about the rest of my cleaning. I didn't feel I had overstepped my boundaries, as my boss had previously informed me about his writings, plus the papers were open on the dining room table.

I believe God put me in this house for this new Nanny/housekeeper career and possibly for a career in "writing" also. I was thirty-nine years old and little did I know it, but I was starting a brand new chapter with my Maker in charge. The "dancing chickens" were certainly getting bigger and fatter in my life and they truly were proving to be abundant, divine blessings.

That night I went home, sat down after supper at the kitchen table and put a poem on paper. Not only was it quite quickly done but it rhymed and made sense.

Jesus put me in THAT house for more than one reason and the reasons were beginning to produce fruit.

Dear God, your Holy Word says that you have a plan for each one of your children and, I thank-you for your beautiful plan for me.

As the next couple of years unfolded, I just kept writing. I found my poems were mostly about special relationships that I believe every single person has at least some of. God's Holy love presence was felt in each verse, so I called it "Soft Christian Poetry".

After two years at my first Nanny/housekeeper position, I was hired by another family, with this time, two little boys. I started in August 1998, again for another teacher and business man. This time I was there for almost three years.

As their Nanny, I also kept writing. I soon had 100 heartfelt relationship poems. During my years writing poems I also wrote and illustrated many children's story books.

It was after a couple years of writing that I decided I would try to share them with the public. I ended up renting a table at the farmer's market within our fair city. My poems were the retail merchandise put on fancy paper and laminated for durability. Many laminated poems were placed in decorated frames and each was sold as gifts to give. Many people of all walks of life seemed to enjoy them and were touched by each poems flavor of love.

For six summers I had a wonderful time behind my table, enjoying many happy, familiar and unfamiliar faces. As time progressed I offered to write personal poems for people for a very minimal charge.

God is good, all the time! Never in my life before did I know this gift was in-side of me and praise God, here it was. If I would have died in my first marriage, I never would have had this beautiful experience to behold and enjoy.

As you can see from my story, I went from poverty, destruction, despair and desperation to fulfilling dreams that I never knew existed or were possible. Jesus can and will pick you up out of any black pit you are in and bring love, life and fulfillment, if you only believe by asking Jesus into your heart. By asking His forgiveness of our sins, then telling publically someone of your decision to follow Him, then trusting His written Holy Word, the Bible, your name also will be written in the Holy Book of Lambs, up in Heaven. That means life, abundantly, now and for eternity is yours for the receiving. Your broken life, here on earth, can be rebuilt and you too can soar like an eagle and produce fruit that is sweet and nourishing.

Chapter 46

Mackenzie is rescued!

Another huge "dancing chicken" that saved the life of my eldest son, Mackenzie, was indeed only a miracle that Jesus, God the Father and the Holy Spirit could do.

Stories of Jesus in the New Testament of the Bible, tell us of Christ bringing healing to many people and also bringing many people to life again, after being pronounced dead. That was then and Jesus has proven to me, that can happen, now also in our time.

When my oldest son, Mackenzie turned thirteen, he decided to go live with his father. It was April of 1995 and Mackenzie approached me in the kitchen about his wanted move.

At first I was horrified and in shock but somehow, when I heard Mackenzie's timid courage, I was somewhat relieved because I too knew his father could better afford the, necessary needs of my growing young sons.

Even though money in our home was very limited, my

heart ached at the painful thought of either of my children leaving me. And little did I know, at that present time, that the move away from me may end up being very costly to my very own children.

As much as I loved deeply my two boys, children from birth, I knew financially I was totally unable to support them properly since the divorce. Because of my nervous break down and my lack of being financially well, I only felt my undying true motherly love and obligation towards them.

I believed in my heart, mind and soul, that always, I am their mother. As young children I gave them every moment of my life, every fiber of my emotions, time and love. I breast fed them as infants, cared for their every need possible and now I prayed, that if I loved them enough, I would have to give them "away" for a period of time, for my two beautiful boys to "come back" to me again, in time.

With the conversation over, the decision made, we made plans for the move and soon our house was almost children empty. Within weeks thereafter, Mackenzie and Kirby had made their move to their new home.

The summer came, the summer went, school started and by Christmas, my once healthy, sturdy son was now much thinner and fighting troubles with his bowels. He had never experienced intestine discomfort before in his life or when he was residing with me. What was going on? What had happened? God only knows for sure. Christ had saved my life and little did I know it then but God was going to save Mackenzie's life also.

Mackenzie and Kirby continued to live with their dad

but Mackenzie's condition only worsened. He got slighter and slighter as he ate less.

My youngest son, Kirby, during this time, I noticed one day at our house, had no eye lashes. Again, what was happening to my boys? Mackenzie apparently had conceived colitis and Kirby had been pulling out all his eye lashes.

The first thing I did was go to my family doctor, trying to get answers to these troubling questions. Why were my sons experiencing such drastic irregularities with their health?

There at the doctor's office, my doctor of many years, read to me from his doctor's medical book that both conditions were probably caused from stress and bad nerves.

I knew I had almost died, expired, given up the ghost, also because of negativity, stress and mainly because of lack of love, while married in that house. Now it seemed my children were experiencing something negative causing sickness also.

I asked the doctor for a photo copy of the article from the medical journal so I could share this vital information with my ex-husband. I took it straight to his home, knocked on his front door and waited with anxiety for his reaction.

The door opened and I addressed the reason for my visit. I showed him the pictures and medical write-up only to be again, horrified by a vain, arrogant response which was "My wife is a social worker and she knows better than anyone how to handle Mackenzie and Kirby."

My son's were now suffering and their father was totally in denial of any personal part of the cause. How could a responsible loving father and a professional wife think that they know better than a trained physician? Jesus, please help my children!

Somehow I knew in my soul before I made the visit that I would be met with a closed heart and mind. God forgive these people for such vanity and control, plus please keep Mackenzie and Kirby from harm.

I left his house, with Mackenzie and Kirby, sitting, vulnerably in their father's and step-mother's hands. I knew if I was going to get involved more, with whatever was happening in that house, to my son's, it was going to be a battle. I thought it over and decided that I would have to wait and watch for more negative signs and if necessary, then I could take them to court.

Since I'm not much of a fighter, I prayed and watched.

For months Kirby's eyelashes were gone and Mackenzie's colitis just got worse and worse.

Now both my son's have always been very respectful of both their parent's and people in general. When they resided with me in their young years, they always had manners and very pleasant, calm personalities. They seemed to always stay on the straight and narrow road of life and very seldom had I ever heard either one of them put anyone down. Seldom had I heard a nasty word come from their young mouths.

However, Mackenzie and Kirby continued to live with their father while I kept praying nightly and sometimes during the days, for what I personally knew I could do little about, unless I caused a huge ruckus.

After three or four months, Kirby's anxiety seemed to

abate as his eyebrows slowly grew back. He told me that he cleaned house, vacuumed, dusted, and cleaned bathrooms as part of his house-hold chores. It almost seemed that he was designated the house-keeper for that household. Again, I didn't interfere. I just listened and watched.

As the next few months unfolded, with Kirby's eyebrows growing back, he again seemed to rebound back to a healthier state.

Life went on and even with colitis Mackenzie graduated high school and afterwards got a science degree. He was always very slim and continually doctoring. He then went on to higher schooling and almost finished another degree to supplement the first one.

Away from home and very home-sick, Mackenzie's colitis became very sever but by the grace of God, he was attending university where there also was a University hospital with some of our countries highest trained doctors available.

As the colitis became almost physically unbearable, Mackenzie was advised by his doctors, to remove his large intestines surgically. If he didn't have the operation, he was told, he would be risking cancer. He was so tall and slight, in body weight that, he reminded me vividly of when I was a walking skeleton, almost dead person. This painful memory caused with-in me to hate the thought of his suffering and to know too well, that his young life could be at stake like mine was. It was as if an another enormous "flying monkey" was looking me right in the face, only this time "it" was after my son.

It was on a Monday morning in the middle of winter

and Mackenzie's surgery date had come. I had no physical way of being in the far off city, where my son was laying in a hospital bed, at a crossroads in his short life, in one of our countries best qualified hospitals.

I knew it was a very serious operation but somehow, God please forgive me, again, I couldn't find transportation to be there with him. Mackenzie's dad and step-mom had driven up to the University Hospital, three hours away and I ended up going to work.

Chapter 47

The Operation

Monday morning 9:00 a.m., operation day, I sat at my place within the elementary school classroom feeling numb and empty. I was there in body but my whole emotional being was certainly not. School duty was the last thing on my mind and as we all sat in circle time, first thing that morning, I looked up at the clock and out loud told the circle of children and fellow teachers that my oldest son, Mackenzie, at that moment was going in for surgery to remove his large intestines.

The words had not completely left my lips when, with crippling emotions, I was flooded with tears and physically was overthrown with despair. The next fifteen minutes were unbearable and the classroom teacher couldn't help feel my intense pain so I was sent home. The moment I got home I called Randall at work. I told him I HAD to go to Mackenzie. My husband was very distraught over this horrible situation but knew it would be almost impossible for him to get away from his commitments at work.

Hanging up one line, I then phoned my brother, Jonathan. After telling him the emergency situation crumbling before me, he agreed to take me, with-in the hour, to my son, who was three hours away and in surgery. He warned me, however, that he had to come back the same night because he too, had obligations at work the next day that also were unavoidable.

At this point I didn't care. I just needed a ride up and back and my brother, Jonathan was it! I needed beyond description, to see my son! I felt I had let things go or allowed things to happen up until now because no one in that family would listen to me but now I knew I needed to be there myself. This "flying monkey" was not going to take my son's life if I had anything to say about it. My Jesus had proven to me many times in my life that He is a God full of "saving miracles" and I just knew Mackenzie could be saved but I also knew I had to be there at Mackenzie's side, to tell him that Jesus loves him and so do I, his mother.

The morning operation was over, Mackenzie was in the recovery room and we arrived at the hospital. My son was alive! He had made it through the operation! Thank you, Lord.

A couple hours later the nurses brought him back into his room and I had a few moments alone with him. He seemed calm and unshaken of his situation. He showed no sign of fear or anxiety. He was totally conscience, yet numbed of expression.

As his mother, I only saw God's grace on his handsome face while I told him that I had been praying for his wellness and also believing he would rebound from this sickly illness and invading operation. He didn't fight me, he just listened. Since his dad had rejected so severely any of my spirituality earlier in life, I knew I could only talk to Mackenzie in private. With Mackenzie being born of my womb, I knew he had some of my blood in his veins also and I prayed he would believe in God's wonders along side of me.

Within hours after the first surgery, Mackenzie was experiencing trouble. Something was going wrong! Again another "flying monkey" was attacking my son. Mackenzie was beginning to drown inside his chest walls and time was of the essence.

God forbid this attack! I squeezed Mackenzie's hand once more and told him that I am very proud of him and I would continue to pray for him. I said a silent prayer and touched his sweet innocent face. Then the family was scooted out of the hospital room and Mackenzie was rushed without delay back into surgery.

The afternoon was waning and my brother, Jonathan began insisting that we had to make our return trip home. He had to be at work by 6:00 a.m. and we still had three hours of driving. I had no choice. There was no possible way I could stay with my son. I had no extra clothes, no where to stay, and no transportation. Again I was in a helpless situation, but I knew Jesus was with me and therefore, with Mackenzie also.

Three hours later Jonathan dropped me off at my front

door in our small town. Immediately inside the house I took telephone in hand and dialed the University Hospital, miles away, to enquire of Mackenzie's operation. It was ten o'clock at night and the nurse told me that the operation was not yet over but I could call back in the early morning.

Somehow, as a Born Again Christian and mother of this child, I felt and knew in my spirit the severity of this second operation and possible outcome. My Spirit was very heavy with a black cloud looming over me and I again felt compelled to petition the Lord, Jesus and Father God Almighty as once before in my life, I was lead to do. Now for my son, I began to pray, plead, cry and plead, pray and cry some more. I needed God the Father to hear my petitions. I needed a miracle for my baby. I knew beyond any doubt that ONLY God's miraculous, guiding hand intervening on Mackenzie's behalf could save his life. I prayed for God to lead and guide the surgeon's hands and to give them wisdom. I began petitioning, Jesus, as soon as I hung up the phone with the nurse. I crawled into bed, only to find myself prostate, face down crying and pleading for a healing miracle. Many hours later I cried and prayed myself, emotionally spent, to sleep only to awaken at 8:00 a.m. the next morning.

With in minutes of wakening, I dialed the University Hospital and after a couple of rings a nurse answered. I questioned her of Mackenzie, telling her I was his mother, and by the Grace of God, she was kind and informative. She continued to tell me that Mackenzie's father and stepmother were called into the intensive care unit at about

12:00 o'clock, midnight, because the doctors thought Mackenzie was going to expire in the next few hours.

My heart was motionless as I waited to hear the rest of her story. Then the nurse went on to say that somehow, Mackenzie's dynamics somehow turned around and sometime in the next three hours an amazing turnaround unfolded. By 7:00 o'clock a.m. Mackenzie had fought his "flying monkey", stabilized and was taken from the intensive care unit to a recovery room.

Again, Praise my precious Jesus! Jesus the Physician, again, miraculously answered my petitions! God saved my son! People can call it whatever they want but I know Mackenzie was given a second chance and I, humbly, will always love The God of the Universe for His undying love and power!

I also know God's Holy Word is Truth and the Bible say's God had a purpose for every single person and now God was showing Mackenzie that he too had a purpose to fulfill on this earth. Again, Praise the Lord! Thank you, Father God, from the bottom of my heart.

Mackenzie continued to respond stronger and healthier day by day. In weeks he was transported to our smaller cities hospital where he was only for a short stay longer. When Mackenzie got out of the hospital, he went home with his father.

At the same time I learned that Mackenzie was in a educational position to get his second degree if he only took the final exams. When I heard of him considering this feat, I, at first thought, "no". He's been through enough already! But again, looking back, I see that Jesus had full control of Mackenzie and his life! Praises to the Highest! Maker and Creator, thank-you!

Within the next few weeks, maybe three, Mackenzie took up pen and paper. He wrote his final exams, only to pass and receive a second degree which gave him the credentials to be a "Health Inspector".

Glorious Father, now Mackenzie, my precious son, was possibly going to be put in charge to help large groups of people stay healthy within eating establishments.

Oh my loving Father, how faithful You are!

This very special event in my son's and my life make me reflect back to Dec 7, 1988, when I petitioned the Lord the first time. The scripture that God gave me was, "If you leave mother, father, your spouse or children because of my name's sake, I will one hundred fold bless you back." "Put God your Father first in your life, not even your children first and you will be blessed!"

Now many years later, after that choice of faith, my undying, ever faithful Holy Father God, Jesus, God's Son, and The Holy Spirit, is again saving physical lives with in and outside my circle.

Gracious King, only you are worthy to be praised!

Mackenzie's health continued to get better and better. He applied to some large cities for the position of "health inspector" and as I write this, Mackenzie has been an official Health Inspector for a very large city for almost three years! He is colitis free and not just existing but living a full and rich texture of life, even without his large intestines.

I believe from different conversations with my son, that

he is doing right now what God Almighty Himself ordained Mackenzie to do! With proof "in the pudding", as to say, God has proven once more of His truthful Word of a purpose for every single person on earth.

Chapter 48

My Pension

Fifteen years of marriage bliss in my second marriage and I was in for another amazing "dancing chicken" that God put into action, actually on the date of my divorce finalization, sixteen years previous.

In my extreme unhealthy and poverty stricken state, sixteen years earlier, I did not want to fight for material things. All I wanted was my freedom from daily negative controlling, a Godless living environment and to raise my two beautiful sons.

It so happened that my exceedingly successful divorce lawyer, whom truly was awesome, fired me because I didn't want to abuse Murrey financially or take him to the cleaners and or destroy him financially. The Holy Spirit had guided me within the lawyer's office, not to fight for material assets like my house, alimony, RRSP's and the proper child support.

Therefore, I didn't and my lawyer was gravely disappointed with me. She accepted my wishes but deep down I think she was quite angry with me.

Within a month before the divorce date, Murrey had spoken to me about speeding up the final divorce procedure and since I was so naive, I approached my lawyer. When I approached her and asked how much longer until the divorce settlement, she basically blew up at me with anger in her voice and announced that my case will be assigned to another lawyer outside her office. I was then in an uncomfortable, embarrassing position and my fate transferred elsewhere.

Murrey learned of this happening and then proceeded with his lawyer to divorce me. The final judgment ended up that our "paid for" home would be sold. My ex-father-in-law that had previously, over an eight year period, had given us six thousand dollars towards our mortgage as a gift, was taking $24,000.00 from the sale. The house sold for $65,000.00 subtract the real estate agents and lawyers $5,000.00 fees, minus $24,000.00 to Murrey's dad. That left $36,000.00 to divide between Murrey and me which was $18,000.00 for each of us out of a $65,000.00 paid for home.

With most of the money going to Murrey and his father, I was pushed into a state of poverty with no money for a down payment for a house because I only had $400.00 a month college employment income which was not enough to make house payments.

Since my car was twelve years old and literally falling apart I decided to purchase a smaller newer car out of reasons of need. The cost of gasoline would be less and the vehicle reliability hopefully would be higher.

Murrey had agreed to pay monthly child support money's of $150.00 per child while most other child support payments from other father's were $300.00 per child. Because I didn't fight for more of anything, I was pushed aggressively into deep poverty.

With Murrey's legal actions of trying to destroy my very being and rape me financially, he did agree, however, of one financial fairness agreement, that Murrey and his lawyer put into the divorce settlement.

Since I had come so close to death on one occasion early in life, I believe Murrey thought that, his agreement applying to the future years of payable pension to me, would never come to be enforced because he thought I would not live long enough to receive it.

He, himself, put in print and agreed to pay me my share of his work pension, on his retirement. Since I basically got nothing from the divorce settlement he pretended to act humanly for my future, with his lawyer's advice.

My first marriage lasted fourteen years and I had nothing financially to show for it, except by the Grace of God, I at least had custody of my two beautiful children at my side and a faithful God leading me through whatever, was coming my way.

In my new life, with lots of new friends and family, I am loved for my hearts content and not for my money. Fifteen years had passed of my new marriage and the old divorce pension contract came due. Now Murrey was in for a little surprise.

I took the written divorce agreement to my lawyer and proceeded to put in a claim on my now payable pension portion.

Praise God! Years later, I found out at that my ex-husband's lawyer of sixteen years ago was and is also a Christian man and again God proved to be in control. God used Murrey's own lawyer, also a man of God, to give me some kind of fairness in a very unfair, humiliating situation.

As the years unfolded, I still prayed every night before sleeping, as my total being was slowly healing inside and out. The Holy Spirit kept leading and guiding me as my life became full of many "dancing chickens" of all shapes and sizes.

One of the most healing prayers I prayed, that healed my soul of hatred, for what Murrey had so cruelly done to me, weather intentionally or by fate, was, "Vengeance is God's, not mine, sayith the Lord."

Every night for the first ten years or so of my new marriage, I would repeat, while nightly praying, this scripture while emotionally putting my toxic anger on Jesus' shoulders and relaxing. Just a drop at a time, His great and mighty promises took my pain and hatred. God does not want us to live with the crippling disease of hatred burning deep within our hearts. It only destroys us with more physical or mental disease of other kinds. Our very happiness depends on forgiveness.

I would always also lift up Murrey's whole nuclear family to my heavenly Father and slowly but surely, by the Grace of God, the pain of hatred dissolved and I was once again free. Now I still lift them up, but not in anger. I lift them up because they need Salvation. God loves them also. God saved me, in so many ways and the least I can do, to thank Jesus, is to pray for my children's dad and family, for their revelation of Salvation.

Not only did I live to receive my pension, I am healthy and free from bitterness. Thank you, Jesus for your faithfulness and Holy Book of promises.

And yes, when I applied for my pension, my ex-husband tried to fight the divorce agreement that many years earlier he put there in print, only this time, the outcome was for Murrey to lose.

Jesus knew that if I trusted Him, I would be blessed by my very own once spiritual enemy called my ex-husband.

Chapter 49

In conclusion of this turbulent road in my life, I believe, as a Born Again Believer, I have learned many spiritual and earthly truths that are true and exceedingly educational. I have heard it stated that "life" is a school and within it are many, many lessons. If we don't learn our life lesson the first time around, I believe the lesson will be repeated.

As we encounter choices, people and events, I believe all we have to do is listen to our hearts as Jesus knocks at our hearts door. We can exchange death for life in the simple act of asking Him into our lives, whether young or old. When praying while trusting God, our faith will grow according to our earthly steps we take, which in turn will lead us into our fulfilled purpose in life.

Read, listen and learn what the Holy Bible wants to teach us, for if we want to get to know the God that made every star in the sky, than we can, by learning His abundant joyful promises and rules to live by. Over time and obedience we can also have a full abundant life's journey. Jesus loves us and is in the miracle business.

I have learned through trial and error that the ten commandment's and contents of the Bible are not for God's benefit but they have been written for yours and mine. We are the benefactors of God's divine plan which is everlasting eternal life, with Him, which starts the moment you ask Christ into your heart, here on earth.

I believe it is our Father in Heaven that puts dreams and challenges with-in our hearts to, moment by moment, year by year, shape and sculpture us into the best equipped person we can be. With the Holy Spirit, who is gentle and kind, we can realize and experience the overflowing joy and love, in every circumstance we experience in life.

Chapter 50

In Conclusion

Now twenty-four year's later, after my living body almost died, I am triumphantly still alive. As each day passes, I am still overcoming obstacles but through God's complete faithfulness, my faith has grown leaps and bounds by the evidence of a living Savior. It seems that daily I am witnessing miracles and wonders within my life, in lives I pray for and other praying Christians.

I know beyond a doubt that the adventure and rescue that is ever present in my life, is without a doubt, available for all other people, young and old. That simple prayer I said so many years ago, asking Jesus for forgiveness and to come into my heart, was by far the most important thing, in my life, that I have ever done! That simple, yet huge, decision is the foundation of my meaningful, joy filled world of unending, caring relationships, both with numerous, family members and friends.

My new husband of over 18 year's, is totally the absolute best friend I could ever ask for. Our four beautiful children are over comers, living full abundant lives in their choice of work field.

Our oldest son, Mackenzie is still working as a "health inspector" for a large city. Our second son, Ryan, with his wife, Jenny, has excelled to become a "master's electrician" in a large city centre. Our youngest son, Kirby, has chosen the career field of employment as a city "police officer" in yet another large city. And finally, our only daughter, Laurie, with her husband, Nickolas, has chosen the field of retail, within a large international chain of outlets. She and her husband have also given Randall and me our first grandson, Simon.

Our family was truly at a turbulent, difficult place nineteen years ago, but as time unfolded, God's guiding hand, nurtured us slowly but steadily bringing love and success to each and every one of our family members.

If you would like that never ending love in your life, but didn't know how to get it, please consider right now to become a new person, starting on the inside, working out.

Don't let those "flying monkey's" destroy your life. Ask Jesus into your heart and daily life. Ask for His forgiveness. Know His promises are real, for He is just waiting for the opportunity to be your best friend. Let Jesus prove to you, that He loves you.

From the bottom of my heart, may God bless each one of you richly, now, through this life and all eternity!

In Jesus Name

Elizabeth Storres

P.S. One thing I'd like to make clear is that my story is not to disrespect any person living or dead. My complete intent is to glorify God the Father, Jesus His Son, and The Holy Spirit by sharing just some of the incredible miracles experienced in my life.

From the bottom of my heart, Be Blessed Always!